EVEN BETTER MATHEMATICS

Looking back to move forward

Afzal Ahmed and Honor Williams

**network
continuum**

Network Continuum Education
The Tower Building
11 York Road
London
SE1 7NX

80 Maiden Lane, Suite 704
New York, NY 10038

www.networkcontinuum.co.uk
www.continuumbooks.com

An imprint of The Continuum International Publishing Group Ltd

First published 2007

ISBN: 1 855 39147 3 (paperback)

Library of Congress Cataloging-in-Publication Data

Ahmed, Afzal.
   Even better mathematics: looking back to move forward/Afzal Ahmed and Honor Williams.
– 1st ed.
      p. cm.
   Includes bibliographical references and index.
   ISBN 978-1-85539-147-5
   1. Mathematics – Study and teaching – Research.   2. Curriculum planning – Research.
   I. Williams, Honor.   II. Title.
QA11.2.A36 2007
510.71-dc22
                                                                                        2007029517

Typeset by BookEns Ltd, Royston, Herts
Printed and bound in Great Britain by

Contents

Acknowledgements

The strength of the Low Attainers in Mathematics Project was in the large number of people who participated in it. These included all teachers, teacher researchers, teachers on diploma courses based at West Sussex Institute of Higher Education (now the University of Chichester) and those in support and other working groups throughout the six project local authorities. It also includes those pupils, parents, employers and others who were involved with the project's work.

It would be impossible to list all these people separately or describe their particular involvement. We wish, however, to acknowledge specifically the contribution of the teacher researchers, West Sussex Institute of Higher Education staff, LA mathematics advisers and the Steering Committee for their active and continuous involvement over the three years; these are listed in the original report, *Better Mathematics*.

With respect to the original report itself we are particularly grateful to those listed below.

The large number of individuals and groups for their time and commitment in responding to draft chapters of the report either through using them as in-service resources or through commenting on their substance. The feedback gained was an integral part of the production of the report.

John Rickwood, technical director of Gower Consultants Ltd, for his many contributions. The fact that from his business perspective he was able to support the outcomes and to identify with the concerns of the project's work through creating and drawing the original cartoons has been of great value.

Frankie Sulke and John Mitchell for the time invested by them in shaping and structuring the report from all the collated evidence.

Even Better Mathematics would not have come about without Jim Houghton, the managing director of Network Educational Press (now Network Continuum Education). We are indebted to him for initiating this writing and for his encouragement, perseverance and patience.

Foreword

This book is based on *Better Mathematics* (1987), the report of the Low Attainers in Mathematics Project (LAMP) (1983–86). LAMP was one of three post-Cockcroft Department of Education and Science (DES) studies related to low attainers in mathematics. The project was based at the Mathematics Centre, West Sussex Institute of Higher Education (now the University of Chichester). The funding bodies were the DES and the local authorities of Dorset, East Sussex, Hampshire, Isle of Wight, Surrey and West Sussex, and West Sussex Institute of Higher Education.

So why now?

The French phrase, *Plus ça change, plus c'est la même chose* (the more things change, the more they stay the same), may not seem plausible when we know that life is always in a state of flux. The periodic appearance of the 'back to basics' movement in education, in different guises and contexts, to oppose the emergence of the so-called 'liberal movement' of offering pupils and students active involvement and enjoyment in their own learning, is a good example. Similarly, the employer and higher education criticisms of pupils who have obtained good examination results not being able to think independently, communicate, make decisions and so on also keep returning at regular intervals. The many attempts to respond to this criticism in various forms are manifested in initiatives such as core skills, thinking skills, problem-solving skills, functional literacy, creativity, emotional intelligence and so on.

It does not take an intensive literature search to uncover that circumstances change and the knowledge base increases but the fundamental ideas about the way human beings learn remain consistent. These ideas have been articulated by philosophers and educationists such as Socrates, Rousseau, Piaget and Dewey and in various learning theories over a long period. What appears as dramatic social and institutional changes around us are often a part of the action–reaction cycle described above and which is bound to continue.

At the end of 2006, Professor Marcus du Sautoy gave the Royal Society 2006 Christmas lectures. He is quoted in *The Times* 23 December 2006 under the headline 'Professor calls for inspiring teaching' as saying,

> 'Pupils often get very bored with the first stage of secondary school maths. There is too much emphasis on numbers and sums. People think that maths should be all about arithmetic, but that is wrong. We don't excite children with maths at this age. There is almost a fear that we shouldn't expose them to too much "big maths" because they wouldn't be able to take it.'

Better Mathematics,[1] the official report of the project, was published in 1987. Since then, an unprecedented number of initiatives and resources have been developed to help improve mathematics in schools. However, our conviction, supported by a large number of teachers and educators, is that the essential ideas and approaches in *Better Mathematics* are currently more relevant than ever. This book, while preserving the original work, offers another opportunity for all interested in the teaching and learning of mathematics in schools to engage with the core issues in *Better Mathematics* in the current context.

What was the 'Cockcroft Report' and have the core issues changed?

The Committee of Inquiry into the Teaching of Mathematics in Schools was set up under the chair of Dr W. H. Cockcroft (known as the Cockcroft Committee) and worked from 1978–81. This was the government's response to the report published by the Education, Arts and Home Office Sub-Committee of the British Parliamentary Expenditure Committee in July 1977, which listed a range of concerns about the mathematical attainment of children,

'It is clear from the points which are made over and over again by witnesses that there is a large number of questions about the mathematical attainments of children which need much more careful analysis than we have ever been able to give during our enquiry.'

Therefore, the decision to set up a national committee was accompanied by the brief 'to consider the teaching of mathematics in primary and secondary schools in England and Wales, with particular regard to its effectiveness and intelligibility and to the match between the mathematical curriculum and the skills required in further education, employment and adult life generally'. The Cockcroft Committee published the report, *Mathematics Counts*[2] and presented its report to the Secretaries of State for England and Wales on 10 November 1981. The Secretaries in their Foreword to the report wrote,

'Few subjects in the school curriculum are as important to the future of the nation as mathematics; and few have been the subject of more comments and criticism in recent years.'

The concerns about standards in school mathematics as well as a shortage of mathematicians never seem to go away and mathematics also takes a 'centre stage' in any public debate concerning standards in education, nationally and internationally.

In February 2004, over 25 years since the Cockcroft Inquiry was set up, the report 'Making Mathematics Count' was published.[3] In his letter to the Secretary of State for Education and Skills, Professor Adrian Smith wrote,

'Mathematics is of central importance to modern society. It provides the language of analytical tools underpinning much of our scientific and industrial research and development. Mathematical concepts, models and techniques are also key to many vital areas of knowledge economy, including the finance and ICT industries. Mathematics is crucially important, too, for the employment opportunities and achievements of individual citizens. The Inquiry has therefore found it deeply disturbing that so many important stakeholders believe there to be crisis in the teaching and learning of mathematics in England.'

The Smith Report focused on three areas of concern including a long-term decline in the numbers of young people continuing to study mathematics post-16 and drew attention to the following factors underlying this decline.

- The perceived poor quality of the teaching and learning experience.

- The perceived relative difficulty of the subject.

- The failure of the curriculum to excite interest and provide appropriate motivation.

- The lack of awareness of the importance of mathematical skills for future career options and advancement.

  (para 0.13, page 3)

The Foreword of the *The Science, Technology, Engineering and Mathematics (STEM) Programme Report* (2006)[4] gave a pledge to strengthen the UK sciences base, setting clear aims for improving the stock and flow of skilled scientists, technologists, engineers and mathematicians and introducing measures across the educational system to support this.

If changes in the teaching and assessment of mathematics come about as a result of the current surge of initiatives outlined above and many more not discussed here, we cannot be sure that another 'reaction' may not be brewing up.

A background to LAMP – the Low Attainers in Mathematics Project 1983–86

The project LAMP, a follow-up of the Cockcroft Inquiry (1982), was charged in the first instance with the task of developing and encouraging 'good practice' in the teaching of mathematics to low-attaining pupils and then to investigate methods of disseminating its findings. It became clear at an early stage that low attainment was not only a problem for pupils in the 'bottom 40%' attainment range. For example, many teachers expressed concerns that their sixth formers (16–19 years) did not fulfil their potential in the subject in terms of their ability to transfer and apply mathematics. Teachers involved in the project have written about the relevance of the work they were doing in their classrooms with all the pupils they taught. They found the changes they were making in their teaching approaches encouraged all pupils to become more involved in their mathematics and to surpass traditional expectations at every level. The problem became one of underachievement across the whole age and ability range.

The *Better Mathematics* report was based on the work of about 200 teachers who over the period of three years were released from their classrooms for one day a week for at least one out of the three years. The teachers concentrated on improving their pupils' achievement, attitudes, confidence and interest in mathematics. LAMP was further disseminated and developed through *The Raising Achievement in Mathematics Project* (RAMP) (1986–89) in 34 local authorities in five regions in England.[5]

If an action–reaction cycle is an inevitable part of the renewal process of life, the need for a sturdy teaching force able to continuously reflect on their practice is vital. *Even Better Mathematics* offers continuous professional development tools that help improve practice and pupil learning in the context of mathematics, by focusing on systems and cultures that make these outcomes possible. Teachers of other subject area, could also benefit by adapting it for their own field of interest.

Even Better Mathematics (hence referred to as the 'report') aims to offer an insight into the reasons for the recurrent public focus on mathematics as well as a way to address some of the issues. In doing so, it utilizes the experiences and reflections of the key stakeholders, teachers and pupils. Instead of offering prescriptions, it invites the interested readers to actively participate in and reflect on their and others' concerns and hence add clarity to their solutions, in context, which will help to raise pupil achievement in mathematics.

Afzal Ahmed and Honor Williams
March 2007

ENDNOTES

1   Ahmed, A. (Project Director) (1987) *Better Mathematics – A Curriculum Development Study*, London: HMSO
2   Cockcroft, W. H. (Chairman) (1982) *Mathematics Counts: Report of the Committee of Enquiry*, London: HMSO
3   Smith, A. (Chairman) (2004) *Making Mathematics Count –The Report of Professor Adrian Smith's Inquiry into Post-14 Mathematics Education*, London: The Stationery Office
4   STEM (2006) *The Science, Technology, Engineering and Mathematics Programme Report*, London: Department for Education and Skills
5   Ahmed, A. and Williams, H. (Project Directors) (1992) *The Raising Achievement in Mathematics Project – A Curriculum Development Research Project*: Bognor Regis, WSIHE (published by permission of the Controller of HMSO)

Chapter 1

Introduction

Questions and remarks of the following kind surface as soon as issues relating to mathematics teaching and learning are discussed, and it is therefore not surprising that these issues were central concerns in the work of the Low Attainers in Mathematics Project (LAMP).

'It's all been said before. Why don't things change?'

'Why do so many mathematics initiatives have such a short life, whereas some textbooks go on forever?'

'It's all right in theory, but it couldn't happen in my school.'

'There are plenty of ideas and resources around. Why are they so little used?'

'Why doesn't educational research help children more in the classroom?'

'Why do "ordinary" teachers who start to work together on projects and courses immediately become reclassified as "special" teachers?'

'Why does a child say, "But I can't do fractions Miss!", as soon as the title is put on the board?'

'Yes, but what about: the syllabus, my head, examinations, parents, employers, under-qualified teachers, newly qualified teachers, my head of department, lack of resources, large classes?'

Specific concerns, such as the problem of girls and mathematics, and the use of computers in mathematics, important as they are, did not emerge as different in essence from the project's general concern to improve the quality of pupils' mathematics. Information technology has brought a wealth of new possibilities to the mathematics classroom. They are powerful tools and their implication on syllabus content and approaches are extensive. ICT should not be viewed, however, as an isolated component of the mathematics curriculum. Like other resources, ICT should be seen and used as a vehicle for mathematical enquiry to support the mathematical development of our pupils.

In this Introduction we outline:

A The research process.

B The nature, structure and possible uses of the report to promote dialogue, reflection and action.

SECTION A: The research process

In the original aims of the project, the stress was placed on improving action in the classroom. Phrases such as the following occurred:

> to develop good practice …
> to change attitudes …
> to help to interpret …
> to gain insight …
> to enable pupils to …
> to develop ways of working that …

Classroom life is complex. For the project's aim of improved mathematics teaching and learning to be realized, any action taken has to be embedded within this complex situation. Thus the authority for carrying out research and development lay with teachers in the classroom. It was necessary to sustain the contact with all the day-to-day problems of school life, such as difficult pupils and conditions, report writing, examinations and marking. To step back in the interests of 'objectivity' and to ignore those awkward realities of classroom life would have invalidated both the procedure and the outcomes of the project's work.

The project centred on 12 'teacher-researchers'. These classroom teachers were released by their local authorities for one day a week for the period of the project to work collaboratively both at the Mathematics Centre, West Sussex Institute of Higher Education (now the University of Chichester) and in schools. The six local authorities involved (Dorset, East Sussex, Hampshire, Isle of Wight, Surrey and West Sussex) were enthusiastic to develop this initiative as a powerful means of implementing the ideas and proposals set out in the Cockcroft Report, that is, to improve the quality of teaching and learning mathematics.

The original agreed project aims were to:

1. Encourage teachers to change their attitudes to the ways in which low attainers learn mathematics.

2. Suggest activities which should involve low-attaining pupils in a wider range of mathematics than the usual diet of 'basics'.

3. Provide teachers with ideas and strategies which should enable pupils to change their perceptions of mathematics, encouraging them not to view the subject just as a body of knowledge to be 'passed on' fact by fact.

4. Suggest ways in which teachers can continually gain insight into pupils' mathematics, without having to rely on formal tests.

5. Suggest ways in which pupils can arrive at conventional methods and terminology through their participation in problem-solving activities and investigatory mathematics.

6. Develop ways of working which should enable pupils to see links between mathematics and other subject areas.

7. Suggest ways of working which should help teachers to develop pupils' confidence and independence in handling mathematics.

8. Suggest approaches which should help teachers cope with different rates of learning among low attainers.

The power of convictions in shaping behaviour is strong. If teachers do not believe that their pupils are capable of thinking for themselves, they are unlikely to give them the opportunities to do so. Similarly, if teachers themselves have a restricted view of the subject, their pupils' diet in mathematics lessons will be inadequate. This has been found to be a problem as much with well-qualified mathematicians as with non-specialists. Hence a fundamental prerequisite of all the project's work had been to allow mathematics teachers time to question and challenge the implications of their beliefs. The project's experience showed that without this, attempts to provide schemes, reports or guidelines on the teaching of mathematics were very likely to be misinterpreted or ignored, and at best their effects will be short-lived.

Large numbers of teachers throughout the project authorities were engaged in working with other teachers and with their pupils. (For example, those on past and present courses associated with the Mathematics Centre and those involved in support and working groups in the region.) As a result, the project had a large, varied and growing accumulation of knowledge, writing, publications and experience covering all aspects of the mathematics curriculum. Hence, *all* these teachers became part of the project and their work was an integral part of the research. They too were 'teacher-researchers'. The project provided a focus enabling connections to be made between the various groups, which drew and fed from each other – a cellular growth model of expansion. This necessitated that dissemination was through active personal involvement and contact, ensuring that curriculum development and research were firmly rooted in the personal experiences of teachers in their classrooms.

On the one day of teacher release, the teacher-researchers worked in a number of ways including:

- working together, discussing, sharing and reflecting on classroom experiences both successful and unsuccessful

- working in groups focusing on specific issues, including the examination of a number of previous relevant curriculum development and research projects, both in mathematics and in other curriculum areas

- developing strategies for in-service work in their schools and with other teachers

- exploring mathematical situations and evaluating possible outcomes

- evaluating the effectiveness of commercial resources in the classroom

- exploring the creative use of computers in the mathematics classroom

- working with other teachers on in-service courses

- working with other teachers in their classrooms.

During their four days in school, the teacher-researchers explored possibilities and ideas within their own classrooms, involved their colleagues through discussion and collaborative teaching and kept personal records. An important strategy that the project employed involved individuals writing and talking about their own situations and experiences in a personal and uninhibited way. These 'case studies', narratives and extracts from them proved invaluable to other teachers. By their nature they were not prescriptive. Within each experience there are ingredients that other teachers may identify as being transferable to their own classroom. As a result, they are encouraged to try out ideas with their own pupils. When groups of teachers came together to pool their strategies and experiences, their individual options were increased and useful common features emerged that helped to isolate elements, such as teacher personality, that were not necessarily transferable. Through such discussion and personal experimentation, the processes of questioning, experimenting, reflecting and evaluating became embedded in a teacher's practice. These processes become a continuous research cycle where evaluation leads to further questioning, which leads to further experimentation, reflection, evaluation and so on. For teachers to reflect so intensely on their own classroom practice, beliefs and assumptions, both individually and in working groups, involved a good deal of emotional investment. It became clear that the focus of the project centred on a working process that enables teachers to become more aware, discerning, confident and resourceful. The process also pervaded all the project's in-service work. Further, the strategies it embodied were similar to those employed by teachers in classrooms to facilitate children's mathematical development because pupils also need to be involved in questioning, experimenting, reflecting and evaluating their mathematics in order to become more aware, discerning, confident and resourceful.

SECTION B: The report

The nature of the report

Even Better Mathematics has been structured around the following considerations:

- The report is not 'the project' itself but the distillation of the experiences and knowledge of the large numbers of teacher and others who were involved. Each chapter of the report considers a major focus and emphasis of the project's work and aims to some extent to be self-contained.

- Points considered of particular significance are presented as bold lettered 'statements' and numbered 1 to 35. These statements have been used as generalizations of the project's findings and can be of real help only if teachers involve themselves actively, as illustrated in 'Some ideas for using the report'.

- The report does not use quotations from external sources. All quotations used are from the large body of writing generated by those involved with the project, including teachers, pupils, advisory staff, employers, college staff and parents from six local authorities. The quotations in the report are not simply illustrative. They contain important points and in many ways may be considered the main part of the text.

- The extensive bibliography of useful reading provides the context and materials used as a resource by the project team.

- It was recognized that the report alone could not bring about widespread change in schools. Effective change can only come about by developments that we have described. Ways in which this document might be used as an in-service resource are discussed later.

- Each chapter concludes with a summary outlining the situation and recommendations for action. The recommendations and statements made throughout this report are based on the knowledge and the wide experience of all those who were involved.

Some ideas for using the report

During the original development and writing of *Better Mathematics* (1987), draft chapters were circulated to a large number and a wide variety of people for comment, discussion and feedback. Many of these individuals and groups used them as an in-service resource. Some of the strategies they have used are described below.

- The statements in the report have been used as generalizations to be refuted. For example, a project member wrote about what happened when she used Statement 4.

STATEMENT 4
Mathematics is effectively learned only by experimenting, questioning, reflecting, discovering, inventing and discussing. Thus, for children, mathematics should be a kind of learning which requires a minimum of factual knowledge and a great deal of experience in dealing with situations using particular kinds of thinking skills.

'I offered the teachers the statement and asked them to pinpoint any areas of disagreement. They had to provide concrete, personal examples to back up their point of view. No second-hand stories or myths were allowed.

After some small group discussion, there was a feeling that the word 'only' in the statement was wrong. Many teachers gave their own schooling as examples. They said they had been taught without any experimentation in their schools and yet had learned mathematics effectively.

After some probing and discussion they decided there was more to 'experimentation' and 'discovering' than 'scissors and paste'. They identified that this had often taken place outside class time, with friends, or on their own when experimentation and reflection were internalized.

By the end of the session many wanted the word 'only' underlined, and everyone had benefited from the discussion.'

- Individual chapters have been used as a focus and a stimulus when teachers at all levels have come together to discuss and plan to address specific issues of concern to them.

- Ideas from the chapters have been explored in a variety of ways to provoke thinking and action. For example, in using Chapter 2, 'Children Learning Mathematics', it has been found helpful to invite teachers to make up their own list of 'What makes a rich mathematical activity'. Similarly, much discussion has developed when teachers have compiled their own lists of classroom actions that restrict or facilitate pupils' mathematical development (see Chapter 3, 'Aims and Actions').

There is potential throughout the chapters for developing professional development activities. For example, Chapter 8, 'Evaluating and Assessing Mathematics', refers to a teacher asking pupils for their opinions as to the 'best way of finding out how good they are at mathematics'. Collecting such responses from pupils may well provide a useful starting-point for a departmental session on assessment.

All the starting-points provide a stimulus and focus, enabling those involved to discuss, challenge assumptions, reflect on experiences and plan future actions.

Chapter 2

Children learning mathematics

'A mathematical classroom can leave memories of excited and exciting discussions, of a varied pattern in its patchwork of learning, of fascination in the revelations of number and shape and of deep personal satisfaction in the defeat of a problem.'

(Ministry of Education 1958)

'Scholars will thus be trained at an early age to use their intelligence, and not to place undue reliance upon the mechanical application of general methods.'

(Board of Education 1905)

'Teachers should restrict themselves to giving children facility only in such mathematical skills as they can use and see the point of using.'

(Board of Education 1937)

'Teaching should, in the main, be based upon the child's own experience and previous knowledge and … upon definite experiments made by him with concrete objects.'

(London County Council 1911)

'The exercises in reasoning afforded by arithmetic can have their full value or force only when the child himself investigates and draws inferences – when he fully realizes the conditions of the problem, and is able to search for ways and means of solving it.'

(Monteith 1928)

Statements of this kind have been made for a very long time by those concerned for the mathematical development of children, yet these assertions are still with us and even considered 'innovative' and 'new'. However, it is not difficult to find classrooms where children still:

- lack confidence in the subject

- spend a majority of their time reproducing their teachers' examples with different numbers

- answer only other people's questions

- ask, 'What am I supposed to be doing then?'

- fail to connect their mathematics with other subjects or with their life outside school, even when they are successful in their mathematics lessons

- dislike mathematics, seeing it as irrelevant and boring

- spend most of their time mystified.

Although students on initial teacher training courses may have firm beliefs derived from their own experience about how to encourage mathematics learning, they often undergo a form of 'retraining' when they get into schools where an attitude of 'This is real life, you can forget what they told you during your training' may exist. A newly qualified teacher (NQT) wrote:

'I have started my NQT year with the conviction that I shall strive to make mathematics for my classes like it has been for me at college.

I want the children to experience pushing forward, trying out and modifying their own mathematical thinking rather than merely digesting and subsequently practising other people's smoothed out and polished ideas. I want them to be able to ask their own questions; to cover "content" through their own explorations; to focus on connections and relationships rather than on isolated ideas and skills; to have opportunities to follow up their own interests; to think of actively interpreting other people's mathematics rather than passively absorbing it; to acquire confidence in their own abilities and feel the power of extending and controlling what they do.

But my intentions are frustrated by a range of things. Among others, they include:

- a weekly computation paper which emphasizes what the children cannot do;

- time-consuming form filling which leaves me little time to concentrate on planning how to involve children in inquiring for themselves;

- detailed record sheets of some 80 items all concerned with number, which include things like "Division of hundreds, tens and units by units without exchange".

And the irony is that all this has been thought out with the children's interests firmly at heart!'

Thus, if improvements in the learning of mathematics are to be widespread, it is inevitable that sustained change must begin with teachers themselves. Their beliefs about the nature of mathematics, how children learn and their own role are crucial factors in determining what actually happens in the classroom and therefore in determining the quality of children's mathematical development.

Figure 2.1 contains some pupils' writings on their perceptions of mathematics.

> Mathematics is about learning to do sums and to do fractions and angles
>
> Mathematics is about thinking, its about working things out.
>
> Mathematics is about .... Finding theories and formula to link together certain problems, so as to find an answer to all areas releating to those problems. Finding links and patterns between puzzles and questions, Leading up to a solution, so we can use that formula to work out all releated queries. Mathematics is borderless, and does not just stop at numbers and number releated topics, such as algebra. But shapes, sizes and all sorts of things.
>
> mathematics is about learning how to count, add, subtract, times and divide
>
> mathsmatics strains your brain to the extream
>
> for little children - money and clocks.
>
> It is about learning to find the area of something
>
> Algebra Mesuration, geometry Trigonametry, Graphs, sets, statistics and prabability and calculus.
>
> I think maths is a problem waiting to be answered

Figure 2.1

Mathematics has enjoyed prestige as a subject for a very long time. Sometimes this has bordered on notoriety (try telling people at a party that you teach mathematics), but more often it has been viewed with some awe.

'It's hard and shows that you are clever.'

There is, however, a wide range of definitions as to what mathematics is. Some of these definitions are matters for philosophy, some come down from the perceived needs of industry, science and other disciplines. More of them have historical origins, often in social contexts such as 'public school scholarships' and 'elementary school arithmetic'. Indeed, most people's perceptions of mathematics are shaped by the way they were taught the subject at school.

A lecturer in mathematics wrote of the public's perceptions of his subject:

> 'When pleasurable and effective, mathematics is not easily noticed. It can even be described as common sense. Only when unpleasant is it identified as mathematics.
>
> Coexistent with this notion is that which depicts the "professor of mathematics" as a comic figure, totally unpractical and divorced from reality, unable to cope with directions or small change or timetables or the like.
>
> The contrast with literature and other aspects of science and the arts is striking:
>   Fun/popular/amateur-inventive science IS science.
>   Fun/popular/amateur-inventive mathematics IS NOT "proper" mathematics.'

Mathematics seems to be understood by most people to be a body of established knowledge and procedures – facts and rules. This describes the forms in which we observe mathematics in calculation, proofs and standard methods. However, most mathematicians would see this as a very narrow view of their subject. It denies the value of mathematics as an activity in which to engage. Decision making, experimenting, hypothesizing, generalizing, modelling, communicating, interpreting, proving, symbolizing and pattern finding are all integral parts of that activity. Without engaging in processes such as these, no mathematician would have been able to create the procedures and systems mentioned above in the first place. Obviously in recent years there has been an attempt to break this perception but this is too important to be left only to a select group of people.

A mathematics teacher noted:

> 'I have spent many years in schools, and fairly consistently found that I gain much from teachers of art, of music, of design and technology. I realized that much of their success, and value, was probably due to the fact that they were usually "practising" their subjects – they painted, they played, they designed. I think I am persuaded that it is equally important for mathematics teachers to be doing some mathematics themselves, experiencing some of the pleasures and pains, frustrations and fears, which their classes should also be feeling.'

> **STATEMENT 2**
> Teacher enthusiasm for and personal engagement in the processes of mathematics will greatly enhance the mathematical experience of their pupils.

Because of the unquestioned inclusion of mathematics in the school curriculum, most teachers of the subject are not required to justify its place and purpose to pupils, parents or colleagues. It is often the case that teachers have never had the opportunity to examine and to sharpen their beliefs about the nature of mathematics.

A teacher wrote of his changed perception of the subject:

> 'From my own point of view I have certainly changed my view as to "what is mathematics". I suppose that I had accepted a very restricted view of a number of mathematical topics – the syllabus – rather than considering the processes going on. By syllabus, I suppose I also restricted myself to an "exam" syllabus – my teaching stemmed from there.

> I do feel that because I am changing, because I am realizing the necessity of observing what is happening in the classroom in a real sense, rather than just whether Johnny is managing to get 4 when adding 2 and 2 – because my realization of what mathematics is about is changing, the attitudes adopted by my pupils are changing too.'

We have found that when teachers' perceptions about the nature of mathematics have broadened:

A. Teachers have gained insight into how children learn mathematics.

B. There are radical implications with respect to the teacher's role in the mathematics classroom.

C. Teachers and their pupils have derived more success and pleasure from the subject.

A: How children learn mathematics

Figure 2.2 shows the writing of two pupils.

> I enjoy most problems in Maths because it gives a good challenge for me.

> Some of the problems are a good challenge which I like but if it is too hard you are aloud to make it easyer. I would like Maths to carry on like this next year becouse it make's you think

Figure 2.2

It is often the case that the mathematical diet for low-attaining pupils consists of little more than basic arithmetic, presented in simple step-by-step learning sequences and repeated frequently. This is usually because it is felt that they cannot cope with anything at a higher level or with more demanding work. Many teachers have found, however, that this diet does not enable their pupils to succeed. They find their pupils saying that they do not understand a topic after they have met it over and over again. They find them getting bored with work they have been doing, with varying degrees of success, since primary school. Teachers talk of their pupils' inability to concentrate and their inability to decide which operations to use in different contexts. However, when teachers have presented these pupils with a broader-based mathematical challenge, they have found them actually achieving more. The pupils can cope with the frustration and floundering inherent in such challenges provided it is in a supportive atmosphere or environment, where the process of struggle is viewed as successful in itself.

> **STATEMENT 3**
> In many cases, low attainment is a direct result of the restricted and unfulfilling nature of the work the pupils are given. They need challenges to get their teeth into.

This food analogy was taken further by a university lecturer associated with the project.

FOOD FOR THOUGHT	
Junk Food	**Junk Mathematics**
There is a lot of it about.	See most school textbooks.
All the preparation is done for you by someone else.	This is done by the author or teacher – all the nasties are removed.
The instructions for use are simple and laid out in steps.	See most textbook questions.
It is superficially attractive but turns out to lack flavour.	It looks well structured and appears logical, but is dull and lacks substance.
It does you little good; it tends to pass through quickly.	Pupils are unable to retain or apply it in new contexts.
All the real nutrient is removed and substitutes have to be added.	It offers no real-life situations but invents and contrives them.
DANGER: HEALTH WARNING	
Junk Mathematics can seriously damage your pupils.	

If children are to obtain genuine 'nourishment' from their mathematical diet, it has to be freed from the artificial way in which it is presented. A teacher wrote:

'Generally we interchange (wrongly) learning with remembering, yet if real learning occurred, would we as teachers need to spend so much time on revision programmes? Mathematics has also come to mean right and wrong; there is thus little room for individualized thinking, no room for an opinion. Rules are taught to be remembered. The methods are as archaic as making children recall a 30-line poem – gone is the beauty, the meaning and the enjoyment. All that remains is the fear of forgetting a verse.'

It was certainly the case (in 1983) that in most mathematics lessons pupils were taught rules, technical notations and established conventions of mathematics without acquiring any feeling for why these systems exist. To teach the subject in this way is to obscure the main reasons why people have enjoyed making and using mathematics, and to deny pupils the experience of actually doing mathematics themselves.

The comparisons possible with other areas of the curriculum are enlightening:

- Is drama to be taught from the published text without ever seeing a play, trying to perform one or trying to extemporize or write one?

- Is music to be taught from the score, explaining rules, constructions, notational devices and musical vocabulary without hearing or playing the sound for which the syntax exists?

- Now that we can produce symbolized choreography, do we spend all our time teaching the symbol system so that children will be able to dance when they leave school?

- Are children in art lessons to be taught about different paints and media, and shown other people's paintings without putting brush on paper or hands on clay?

A teacher wrote:

'Relying on a set of rules taught by the teacher is only as good as the child's memory allows for instant and accurate recall. We all know the problem of trying to remember a lot of unrelated facts; they become mixed and muddled for the majority.'

Can we justify the teacher saying things such as:

- 'Line up all the dots and start at the right.'

- 'Take out the decimal point, count the number of numbers behind the point, then stick it back in.'

- 'Two minuses make a plus.'

- 'It's a ten, so we put a nought down first.'

- 'Take it over and change the sign.'

- 'Just add a nought.'

Children must find their own strategies so that they can apply them appropriately and understand established rules for what they are. 'I've forgotten how to do long multiplication' may well mean, 'I've forgotten *your* rule for multiplying two big numbers together'. The more we teach algorithms only, the more inflexible children are likely to become.

A teacher described the following incident with his bottom set, Year 8:

'In this, the second lesson, the children were working on their own variations of a number chain. Mary had decided to *divide* each number by itself instead of multiplying.

I watched from a distance as she dutifully plugged her numbers into a calculator and kept getting the answer 1. She looked genuinely surprised and tried at some very big numbers to test her theory. After that she leapt from her chair and ran to me saying "I've made an incredible discovery! If you divide a number by itself you *ALWAYS* get 1, no matter what number you use."

We then had a discussion about why that should be and it became obvious she really understood. She was so thrilled with this discovery she insisted on explaining it to the rest of the class.

This incident left me both depressed and encouraged. I was depressed because I had assumed from all the division work we had done in Year 7 that Mary already knew that x divided by x is 1. I was encouraged because a) now I am convinced she does know it and therefore won't forget it, and b) that it was the open situation in the classroom that enabled her to experiment and therefore find it out in her way, not mine.'

> STATEMENT 4
> Mathematics is effectively learned only by experimenting, questioning, reflecting, discovering, inventing and discussing. Thus, for children, mathematics should be a kind of learning which requires a minimum of factual knowledge and a great deal of experience in dealing with situations using particular kinds of thinking skills.

B: The teacher's role in the mathematics classroom

Perceptions about children's learning have enormous implications for actions taken by teachers in classrooms.

Consider the following contrasting lists.

List A	List B
• Pupils dislike mathematics and will avoid it if they can.	• Children freely engage in activities that are essentially mathematical.

- Pupils want to be told what to do and be directed towards appropriate tasks.

- Pupils are mainly motivated by teacher approval, a desire to succeed at examinations, or to achieve 'tokens of merit'.

- Most pupils have little creativity or imagination, except when it comes to thinking of excuses for not having done their homework.

- There are identifiable skills that the teacher knows and that need to be explained to the children and practised so that they are well equipped for life.

- Pupils need clear step-by step explanations in order to avoid confusion.

- Pupils are empty vessels waiting to be filled from the teacher's expert stock of knowledge.

- Pupils are able to identify and direct themselves towards appropriate tasks.

- Pupils can become fascinated by mathematical contradictions and absurdities and are motivated by the mathematical activity itself.

- Creativity and ingenuity are widely distributed and evident in the natural activities of children outside school.

- The mastery of skills is of little use if they cannot be applied. The skills pupils need are the strategies of problem solving; interpreting mathematical forms and statements; representing situations mathematically. These must be developed in context, through experience.

- A state of temporary confusion or puzzlement is at the heart of all learning.

- Pupils bring their own knowledge and experience and need to be actively involved in their mathematical development.

The caricature of teacher beliefs in List A would give rise to a correspondingly narrow set of teacher actions, whereas a teacher characterized by List B may well have a wider range of teaching strategies available. The commonly held view that good teachers are ones who can pass on their expertise through clear explanations so as to avoid confusing their pupils has some interesting implications.

- *The view implies that*: the teacher is the holder of answers in a classroom, one who knows the answers to all the pupils' questions. In a classroom where such an answer-oriented atmosphere exists, it is difficult to imagine much exploration into unknown territory taking place, as pupils will find it difficult to believe that there are areas where their teacher does not 'know the answer'. This leads to a marked lack of independence on behalf of pupils as is evidenced by their questions such as, 'Is this right?' or 'Where's the answer book?' This atmosphere also helps to perpetuate the view of mathematics where the only problems are those with a right or wrong answer, or a right or wrong method.

Figure 2.3

- *The view implies that*: the teacher is seen by pupils as having total responsibility for leading and controlling the work that is going on in the classroom. We have found that if pupils rarely get the chance to use their own initiative, they become even more dependent on their teacher for direction. Staffroom complaints about Year 10 still having to be 'spoon fed' are therefore not really surprising. This 'teacher authority' can lead to pupils being stifled by their teachers' expectations.

This teacher highlights the problem:

> 'In developing work in the classroom, one's own expectations and experiences often interfere with a child's progress and it is important to be aware of this and exercise self-control.
>
> My main aim is to direct their work as little as possible, letting them find their own system and choose their own path to follow. I am not advocating no guidance though, since a teacher's role in this respect is a vital one, but it can easily be overdone and destroy a sense of personal achievement.

This requires cutting the instructions to a bare minimum, so that you are, in effect, just providing them with the seed of an idea, and allowing them to cultivate it.'

- *The view implies that*: in a climate of teacher expertise, well-defined methods and careful explanations, teachers often feel obliged to provide clever tricks to short cut the processes of decision making, choice of procedure and securing conviction or proof, often thinking that this is necessary in order to 'get through the syllabus'. Teachers frequently pre-empt pupils' decisions because they do not want them to 'get into a mess'. Their enthusiasm to convey solutions to pupils often ends up by precluding the pupils' own ideas and can be not only inhibiting but also take away the pupils' enjoyment of getting there themselves.

In our efforts to make things easier for our pupils, we often act in other inhibiting ways. Five common classroom actions that restrict pupils' mathematical development are outlined below.

1. *The subject is broken down into 'easily digestible topics'.* Teachers often lament that pupils do not see and use links between different areas of the subject. When it is considered that in the 'real world' mathematics does not come in the small fragmented packages that so frequently exist in our syllabuses (for example, 'perimeter' and 'area'), it is not surprising that pupils are unable to get a useful overview or to see relationships.

2. *There is an over-concern to simplify, by breaking general ideas into seemingly unrelated stages.* The point of the overall task in hand is often obscured when step-by-step instructions are provided; for example, when a pupil neatly sets out a long multiplication sum in order to multiply by 100.

3. *Difficulties are smoothed out for pupils by, for example, ensuring that awkward cases do not occur or that the numbers cancel or that the answer is not a fraction.* This presents a false view of the subject and can lead to a situation where unusual extensions of these easier cases are not recognized. It also restricts opportunities for pupils' own interesting mathematical questions of the following kind:

    'What is infinity plus one?'

    'Is 0 a number?'

    'What's the square root of a minus number then?'

    'What does this symbol mean on my calculator?'

4. *It is often assumed that techniques must be learned and practised before problems are mentioned.* This can lead to a lack of motivation, as well as to a lack of understanding and meaning. When pupils complain that they 'don't see the point of doing all these', they are often given a remote justification – 'You'll need it when you buy a carpet.'

5. *An idea that arises naturally or that has a ready-made context is often unconsciously mystified by over-explanation/exposition.* For example, spending a great deal of time and effort arriving at a rule for rounding off money to the nearest pound. Once again this can lead not only to confusion, but also to a loss of purpose and motivation.

Since the Cockcroft Report (1982), the word 'investigation' has taken on enormous significance in the minds of mathematics teachers across the country. However, in many cases the spirit behind investigative activity in the mathematics classroom has been lost. This is evidenced by teachers asking questions such as 'How much time am I supposed to spend doing investigations?' For them, the word 'investigation' refers not to an attitude pervading all their teaching, but to a new and additional 'topic' to be covered on their syllabus, with identifiable labels such as 'Frogs' or 'Happy Numbers'. If pupils are to benefit, then although activities such as 'Frogs' or 'Happy Numbers' can be excellent starting-points for exploration, it is essential that a spirit of enquiry is seen to permeate the whole of mathematics teaching and learning.

A group of teachers on an in-service course attempted to draw up a list describing necessary ingredients for a rich mathematical activity.

What makes a rich mathematical activity?

- It must be accessible to everyone at the start.
- It needs to allow further challenges and be extendable.
- It should invite children to make decisions.
- It should involve children in speculating, hypothesis making and testing, proving and explaining, reflecting, interpreting.
- It should not restrict pupils from searching in other directions.
- It should promote discussion and communication.
- It should encourage originality/invention.
- It should encourage 'what if' and 'what if not' questions.
- It should have an element of surprise.
- It should be enjoyable.

They then went on to pool ideas on strategies for generating mathematical enquiry.

Start with exploratory-type questions such as:

- How many different …
    ways to work out 21×13?
    ways to satisfy $c = a + 2b$?
    ways to draw an equilateral triangle?
- What happens when …? Can you find a better way …?
    Is it true that …
    12% of £40 is the same as 40% of £12?
- Get pupils to set their own questions
    Then pass them around.
- Ask them to find out how to do something:
    Find the area of a triangle.
    Construct a 30 degree angle.
- Start with a problem or dilemma
    Explore … sort out the contradictions or confusions.

- Start with an answer

    Explore … How did they get it? What was the question/problem?

- What's gone wrong?

    Use an outside stimulus:

    Radio/TV/newspaper

    Puzzles

    Advertisements

    Familiar everyday anomalies.

- Get pupils to make or invent something

    To measure turn

    To measure time

    To carry a certain weight.

- Use games

    Can they make them harder?

    Can they understand each other's rules?

Teachers need to be seen by pupils to be genuinely interested in their mathematical ideas. We have found that this encourages children to ask and answer their own questions. There is a wealth of strategies for enabling pupils to do more of the thinking in mathematics lessons. These strategies were developed further during the Raising Achievement in Mathematics Project (RAMP 1986–89) and are outlined below. The range of possible choices develops when teachers work together, sharing their failures and successes, and pooling their ideas for improving their pupils' mathematical experiences.

Some classroom strategies[1]

- Involve pupils in simple starting-points, then try asking how they might vary these or what questions they could think up to answer next. Collect together pupils' suggestions for variations or questions, perhaps on the board or on a large sheet of paper, and invite them to follow up a suggestion of their choice.

- Ask pupils to keep a record of questions or other ideas they have not attempted. Encourage them to choose one of those questions to work at on appropriate occasions.

- Put examples of pupils' own questions on display. Invite groups to look at and perhaps work on other groups' questions.

- Do not always give pupils rules that work; invite them to try some that do not and to explain why they do not.

- Encourage pupils to find methods and rules for themselves. Involve them in comparing the methods to agree on the most efficient. Try to think of ways of involving pupils in generalizing for themselves.

- When you want pupils to practise skills, think whether it would be possible for such practice to emerge through their own enquiries or problems that will necessitate the use of these skills.

- Think how you might 'twist' tasks and questions described in textbooks, tasks sheets or test papers so that pupils can become more involved in making decisions, describing patterns and relationships and testing conjectures.

- Help pupils to appreciate the importance of asking questions such as 'Is this sensible?' 'Can I check this for myself?' Offer activities that will involve pupils in decisions relating to the 'correctness' of a piece of mathematics.

- Show pupils examples of mistakes. Ask them to sort out what the mistakes are and to think how they might have arisen.

- Consider how you might incorporate the terms and notations that you want pupils to learn, so that meaning can be readily ascribed to them and they can be seen as helpful and necessary.

- Encourage pupils to look for connections between old and new situations, ideas and skills and to ask themselves whether something they did previously might be of use in solving their new problems.

- When a pupil comes up with something that appears initially to be off the track, try to stop yourself from immediately implying that this is the case. What about the possibility of it being kept as a further idea for later.

C: Teachers and their pupils have derived more success and pleasure from the subject

Figure 2.4 contains some pupils' writing (see opposite).

When pupils have engaged in the subject in the ways we indicate in this chapter, they have become more able and willing to understand and tackle established procedures and rules and to sort out mathematical confusions.

Figure 2.5 shows what one pupil wrote.

> I used to be terrible at maths
> These lessons have given me much more confidence and now I understand things better. If somebody gave me a maths problem I would investigate the problem and I would be able to work it out.

Figure 2.5

Teachers who have broadened their range of teaching strategies have found that they are able to overcome the major problem of limiting children's attainment. Pupils at *all* levels surpassed traditional expectations. Examination success and the take up of further courses in mathematics both increased greatly.

Maths is interesting when .... the teacher does not go "waffle, waffle, waffle .. page 64 Exercise A, B, C, D " It's different in this class because we don't just do routine work, we practise something that is very important — thinking

..the bottom set does all sorts of Intresting things and they find out loks of information and I feel so sorry for the top set because they have to copy pages and pages of work out of the maths book

I think it gives us a very good chance to do better. I like it because we are our own boss and we are much more independant. It is much better than staring at the teacher for a lesson or two. That can get terribly boring

When I done pages and pages of work I used to hate and dred going to the less ons. Now I like maths because we solve things

the reason I enjoyed it is because the begining of the work may have been set but then you had the freedom to work on the subject as you wanted to. The thing I learnt most is how to use and the meaning of Mathmatical terms for example the decimal point and fractions

I think I have learnet that the more you find out theres always some thing to go on to

down our old school we allways did sums and you dont really find alot out in sums

Figure 2.4

In the raising of children's attainment and enjoyment, we consider the following five factors significant:

1 Dealing with failure and fear

A teacher wrote:

> 'Mathematics is a subject closely related to failure, and it is also socially acceptable to be bad at mathematics. I think that as long as educated people are not embarrassed but rather proud of their poor levels of competence, then this will not alter.'

It certainly seems absurd that highly educated and successful professionals happily admit that they are 'useless at maths'. The subject is extensively disliked and feared by children regardless of age, ability and background. A teacher commented:

> 'One of my main aims is getting rid of this feeling of fear – fear of asking questions, fear of "getting it wrong".'

When pupils are allowed the opportunities to engage in mathematics as we have indicated, their enjoyment of the subject has increased. When pupils do their own mathematics, it becomes significant for them. Success in such activities is usually very rewarding and includes a strong element of pleasure of the 'I've sorted it out myself' kind. This applies equally to those pupils who already enjoy mathematical activities as well as to those who have been numbed by past experience.

2 Relevance

It is often felt that children will succeed if what they do in the classroom relates to 'everyday life'. While it is true that pupils do achieve more if they see their work as meaningful, the question of relevance is not an easy one, as this teacher points out:

> 'We are preoccupied with relevance, but what does this mean? Relevant to whom, and at what stage? Utilitarian skills are often thought to be important and presumed to be relevant, but do the students perceive them as such?

> Hire purchase calculations are thought to be relevant, but surely this is only so if you are considering purchasing something on HP and even then the salesperson will probably do the calculations for you! I believe that relevance occurs if the student is interested in what he or she is doing. In turn, interest is generated by challenge and variety.'

3 Skills and strategies

If learning is 'effective', pupils should be able to use their mathematical ideas, skills and strategies in a variety of different contexts within the subject, in other curriculum areas and outside school. If children are to be able to cope with the diversity and ambiguity of real-life problems, skills must not be taught in isolation, thus avoiding comments such as 'Is this an add, Miss?' and 'Do I times it first, Sir?'

4 Initiative

A teacher wrote:

> 'The pupils have started to take more responsibility themselves for what we do in the classroom. The work, although initiated by me, is taken through by them to a much greater extent than it used to be and that includes how and where they work. As long as it is done in a sensible manner, they know it will be accepted.'

When pupils are allowed to take decisions for themselves, their organizational skills and initiative are developed and improved.

5 Changing

The changes in mathematics learning and teaching outlined in this chapter are not easy for teachers or pupils, as this teacher emphasizes:

> 'It takes a group some considerable time to develop an enquiring approach. They do not generally expect to think for themselves – to be in a position to make decisions that will govern the directions of their study.'

Changes need to be developed in an atmosphere of mutual trust and confidence. Issues relating to teacher change are considered in Chapter 4, 'Teacher Development'. It is important that, if unnecessary antagonism is to be avoided, pupils are actively involved in implementing changes, and therefore understand what is happening.

Even those who have reached a traditionally high academic level can lack confidence in problem-solving situations and show a marked lack of flexibility when it comes to using their mathematics creatively. Hence they too may be considered 'low attainers' in mathematics.

SUMMARY

The Situation

- General perceptions of school mathematics are exceedingly narrow, and this is a major factor in inhibiting attempts to improve practice.

- Attitudes and practice in mathematics are often markedly different from those in other subjects.

- When teachers' perceptions about the nature of mathematics have broadened, they have gained a greater insight into how children learn mathematics. This has had radical implications with respect to the teacher's role in the mathematics classroom.

- In many cases, low attainment is a direct result of the restricted and unfulfilling nature of the work pupils are given. They need challenges.

- In most mathematics lessons, pupils are taught the rules, technical notations and established conventions of mathematics without acquiring any feeling for why these systems exist. To teach the subject in this way is to obscure the main reasons why people have enjoyed making and using mathematics and to deny pupils the experience of actually doing mathematics themselves.

- The view of a teacher's role being merely to pass on expertise through clear explanations so as to avoid confusion leads directly to:

  a) an answer-oriented atmosphere in the classroom

  b) an overriding dependence on the teacher

  c) the inhibition of pupils' own ideas

  d) a fear of 'getting it wrong'.

- Through pressure since the Cockcroft Report, 'doing investigations' has become in many teachers' eyes another syllabus requirement – a bandwagon – thus losing the spirit behind an investigative approach. An investigative approach to the subject, by its nature, necessitates a variety of teaching situations.

- When pupils are allowed the opportunities to engage in mathematics, their enjoyment, confidence and attainment increase.

- Participatory approaches to mathematics teaching and learning have the potential to improve the attitudes and attainment of all pupils, not just those of limited ability or labelled 'low attainers'.

Recommendations

- Perceptions about the nature of mathematics need to be reviewed and re-examined. This is a fundamental prerequisite to raising pupils' achievement in mathematics.

- For pupils to achieve more, their mathematical diet must encompass challenge and active involvement in directing their own enquiries.

- Mathematics can be effectively learned only by involving pupils in experimenting, questioning, reflecting, discovering, inventing and discussing. Mathematics should be a kind of learning where factual knowledge is acquired through a great deal of experience in dealing with situations using particular kinds of thinking skills.

- Collaborative work between teachers is a major factor in the development of strategies for generating and sustaining rich mathematical activity in the classroom.

- Changes in mathematics learning and teaching may not be easy for teachers or pupils, and must be developed in an atmosphere of mutual trust and confidence.

- It is essential that if the spirit behind enquiry-based learning is to be achieved in our mathematics classroom, then teachers must understand and be in sympathy with the philosophy behind such teaching approaches.

ENDNOTES

1   These strategies have been taken from Ahmed, A. and Williams, H. (1992) *The Raising Achievement in Mathematics Project – A Curriculum Development Research Project*, Bognor Regis: WSIHE and can also be found in Ahmed, A. et al. (2002) *Numeracy Activities, Key Stage 3*, Stafford: Network Educational Press.

Chapter 3

Aims and actions

Enlightened aims in education are not peculiar to modern times. Recent government reports have encouraged the profession generally to consider its aims at all levels. For some time now we have expected local authorities, heads of schools, heads of departments and individual teachers to prepare detailed aims. There seems to be an expectation that these aims will directly influence what happens in the classroom, act as instruments of curriculum changes and form guidelines for teachers in, for example, the production of detailed syllabuses. We have found a frequent mismatch between what is intended by those working in education at all levels and what actions are taken in schools and classrooms. Even when a document sets out recommended actions to implement its aims there is often incompatibility. A letter from a teacher began as follows:

> 'I am both furious and upset! I had worked on basic statistics with my Year 8. Although there is a tight syllabus to keep to, I thought it a worthwhile exercise to get the children to do their own surveys in their homework time over a couple of weeks.
>
> The children got a lot of pleasure from this and spent far longer than they would have on "ordinary" homework – some even going to the lengths of typing out a questionnaire and duplicating it. I got the children to display their work and again many children were quite happy to spend breaks and lunchtimes doing this.
>
> As the walls in my room were already full, the children put up their work in the hall outside and this aroused considerable interest from other children – BUT ... believe it or not my head of department got a note from the headteacher this morning complaining! He had criticized three spelling mistakes – he felt it did not reflect well on the school to have these.'

> **STATEMENT 9**
> Aims for schools, departments and lessons often relate to choice, autonomy, self-motivation and confidence, as well as putting stress on the development of thinking individuals. Actions taken are often incompatible with these aims and sometimes are directly opposed to them.

Figure 3.1

STATEMENT 10
Aims can only act as forces for change and development when those who are to use and understand them are actively involved in either their evolution or in working at their implications as they affect their own situation.

In many instances, the production of a list of aims is a response to a pressure from above, rather than from a perceived internal need. As a result, such aims are often treated unsympathetically and cynically by teachers as products of 'ivory tower thinking' unrelated to the practicalities of classroom life. Without a more meaningful involvement, aims can become misunderstood, misrepresented or even ignored.

Actions can also be at variance with aims when they mask larger 'hidden aims' reflecting ingrained social attitudes towards mathematical teaching. For example, the Cockcroft Committee's recommendation that pupils should be actively involved in discussing their mathematics cannot co-exist with the view that classrooms should always be quiet with pupils working on their own.

The following aims for *Mathematics from 5 to 16* (DES 1985) and some common classroom actions illustrate this mismatch.

AIM

ACTION

'*Mathematics is an essential element of communication.*

The mere manipulation of numerical or algebraic symbols is of secondary importance.'

	a)	b)	c)	d)	e)
1	1.45 × 2	6.83 × 8	19.67 × 7	33.819 × 9	50.267 × 5
2	1.6 × 30	2.8 × 60	29.21 × 90	46.34 × 70	71.142 × 40
3	6.9 × 72	8.3 × 84	9.21 × 43	8.62 × 27	9.53 × 18
4	20.23 × 57	31.65 × 62	8.376 × 94	2.108 × 39	1.663 × 81
5	15.82 × 10	15.82 × 100	15.82 × 1000	1.582 × 100	1.582 × 1000
6	14.6 × 0.2	20.9 × 0.7	15.4 × 1.2	37.9 × 2.3	50.8 × 3.5

'*Mathematics as a powerful tool.*

Skills such as measuring length, telling the time, constructing a graph, drawing geometric shapes, dividing one number by another and solving an equation are not important ends in themselves and only become so as they are embedded in purposeful activities.'

'We must learn about different units so I want you all to measure your exercise books in centimetres, and then when you've done that we can measure the room using metres.'

'*Imagination, initiative and flexibility of mind in mathematics.*

When presented with a mathematical task, pupils should be encouraged to find their own methods of carrying it out even though there may be a standard, more streamlined method which they might ultimately learn.'

'Now, even if you can do it without using the method, I still want you to use it because you'll need to know it for the harder ones later on.'

'The aim should be to show mathematics as a process, as a creative activity in which pupils can be fully involved, and not as an imposed body of knowledge immune to any change or development.'

'Yes, I expect it would work that way, but now let's find out the right way to do it.'

'*Working independently.*

Success in teaching can be gauged, to some extent, by the way in which pupils have learned to work effectively in an independent way.'

'Now when you've finished that make sure you see me to get it marked. Then I'll give you the next bit.'

AIM	ACTION
'In-depth study of mathematics.	
Much of the mathematical experience of most pupils is extremely fragmented, as they proceed from one small item to another in quick succession. An in-depth study is of potential value for all pupils, not only mathematically but also in terms of the development of personal qualities such as commitment and persistence.'	'My pupils can only concentrate for ten minutes at a time so I give them work in small easily digestible topics with easy-to-follow step-by-step instructions.'
'Pupils' confidence in their mathematical abilities.	
Mathematics must be an experience from which pupils derive pleasure and enjoyment.'	'I know you don't like it, but it is on the syllabus, so you'll need it for the exam.'

Mismatch occurs when aims hold no conviction for teachers. Their actions are in fact reflecting their own beliefs about mathematics teaching. These assumptions are reinforced over generations by popular myths relating to good practice in the subject. These powerful 'hidden aims' make it possible for teachers to reject ideas because they don't fit in with how they were taught or because the ideas are at odds with an imagined public view of mathematics and mathematics teaching.

As a further example of the complex relationship between aims and actions, consider the following scenario:

> An educational body concerned with improving pupils' awareness, thinking, communication and decision-making skills sets out a group of laudable aims reflecting the above needs. They want them to be accessible to all teachers and for all teachers to act on them, hence improving the mathematical entitlement of pupils.
> There is concern, however, that teachers will not appreciate or have time to interpret the aims themselves in terms of classroom actions, so a set of guidelines is produced.
> Still little action is taken in schools – teachers are busy marking, preparing, writing reports and have not got the time or inclination to read through the guidelines. In an effort to make it easier for teachers to interpret these guidelines, a checklist of desired actions is produced on which teachers can simply tick off items corresponding to good practice. This is appealing, offering comfort and security.
> When the original aims are presented to teachers, on an occasional in-service day for instance, these are still not recognized. They may also

be seen as irrelevant to their 'school life' and be received at best with indifference, at worst with antagonism and cynicism.

If actions are not to become detached from the original aims, what needs to be done? Aims such as 'helping pupils to develop lively enquiring minds' have been restated in various curriculum documents over generations. Stating them again is not going to help teachers act on them. If we want teachers to use and act on such aims, diluting them into checklists and simple examples does not help either. Indeed, this can lead to the situation where the task of filling in the checklist takes over and becomes an aim in itself.

When actions are seen not to match up with aims, it is often assumed that teachers are not capable or willing to put them into practice. External efforts to remedy this can lead even further away from the original aim. For example, the aim of developing pupils' thinking skills has been implemented in many cases into the teaching of separate 'study skills' lessons. The essence of the original aim, which was to encourage such skills throughout the curriculum, has in many instances been lost as pupils become unable to transfer and apply these skills. A similar problem exists with the 'teaching' of 'life skills'.

We have found that when teachers are involved in working at the implications of aims and their associated actions, these problems are minimized. One of the many in-service activities developed by the project invited teachers to:

a) take an aim they wish to fulfil

b) outline the classroom actions necessary to facilitate the aim

c) consider the consequences or 'prices' of these actions.

When the consequences in c) actually contradicted their original aim, teachers considered further actions to remedy the situation and articulated arguments for the resources and priorities needed. Involvement in group activities of this kind has enabled teachers to productively use reports and curriculum documents previously available but inaccessible to them.

The letter at the beginning of this chapter demonstrates that there is still a problem for teachers attempting to put aims into practice. There will be a vital need for senior management's organizational and moral support especially when teachers may be struggling with new strategies. In addition, senior management also need to be involved as active participants in the process of examining the match between aims and actions.

SUMMARY

The Situation

- Aims for schools, departments and lessons often relate to choice, autonomy, self-motivation and confidence, as well as putting stress on the development of thinking individuals. Actions taken are often incompatible with these aims and sometimes are directly opposed to them.

- There are enormous difficulties with regard to aims being translated into consistent actions.

- In many instances the production of a list of aims is a response to a pressure from above, rather than from a perceived internal need.

- Teachers do not relate to lists of aims in discussion and curriculum documents unless they have been personally involved in either evolving or actively working at the aims and their implications.

- In an effort to simplify aims in order to help teachers interpret and realize them, teacher development is often inhibited.

Recommendations

- Those at all levels in education must be involved in the process of interrogating the implications of aims and their associated actions. This should be an ongoing process and not a one-off activity.

- Senior management must believe in the importance of this teacher involvement and will need to be involved themselves as active participants rather than only as observers or organizers.

Chapter 4

Teacher development

A teacher on an in-service course wrote:

'*My changing thoughts about teaching mathematics to low attainers*

I have chosen the above title to be the subject of my study because I know that unless my thinking about mathematics teaching had been changed – unless I had been personally convinced – there could have been no attendant changes in my classroom practice. That is, without a revolution in my philosophy of teaching mathematics, none of the changes which I am now trying to effect in my classroom teaching could have ever come about.

Furthermore, it is because these new approaches in my helping low attainers understand mathematics are firmly grounded in personal experience and conviction that I feel they will stand the test of time.

If I had merely tried out new methods upon somebody else's recommendation, then in the face of difficulty it would be highly probably that I would just "drop" the ideas. As it is, I sometimes do experience difficulties, and no doubt will in the future, but I know that my underlying convictions will help carry me along.'

The teacher had met similar ideas at college several years previously, but had not tried to implement these in the classroom until recently. She had read the Cockcroft Report but had only focused her attention on the Foundation list of mathematical topics. She developed strategies where pupils can become more confident and involved in their mathematics. The inherent difficulties that she would previously have cited as reasons for not changing are now viewed by her as small hurdles to be negotiated in the course of creating a more worthwhile learning experience for her pupils.

The change in this teacher's behaviour has followed from a change in her convictions.

The power of convictions in shaping behaviour is strong. For instance, teachers who believe that children like and need the security of being told what to do would find it very difficult to put their pupils into a situation where they had to decide what to do for themselves.

The quotes overleaf (see page 34) are from teachers writing about their beliefs.

The quotes overleaf (see page 34)

'The teacher's role is to pass on knowledge.'

'Exam results are the most important factor.'

'Mathematics is not a hierarchical subject – there are many pathways to learning.'

'An examination syllabus should not be used as a teaching syllabus.'

'Pupils will only develop mathematically if they are given opportunities to control their own learning.'

'Mathematics must be taught in a logical order. If pupils do not know how to do the basics, they cannot progress further.'

'The teacher's role should be one of fellow learner.'

'Children like and need the security of being told what to do.'

Through the work of the project it became clear that among teachers' sets of beliefs there are a number of 'dominant' convictions that play a major role in determining behaviour. These beliefs centre around two issues:

a) **The perception of the nature of mathematics:**

'Please Miss, can we do some real maths now?'

It is often the case that teachers have never had the opportunity to examine and sharpen their beliefs in this area and, consequently, they and their pupils do not see thinking, questioning and decision making as integral parts of mathematics.

b) **The nature of learning:**

'We've done it five times already this year and they still don't understand it.'

Beliefs about how children learn are crucial to actions taken by teachers in the classroom.

Dominant beliefs dictate to what extent new ideas will be accepted. When there are strong social pressures to conform, new ideas will be interpreted to fit in with a teacher's existing set of beliefs.

Figure 4.1

Teacher development is a complex, individual learning process and as such needs to be embedded in experience.

The project identified five generalizations that could be made with regard to helping teachers examine their beliefs critically:

1 An element of challenge and risk is essential

A teacher wrote:

> 'The first few months have enabled me to think seriously and deeply about my approach to the subject. It has made me question every aspect of my teaching, including things that I thought I was doing well! Psychologically this has been quite traumatic; but essential. Towards the end of this "shake down" period it has enabled me to experiment confidently, often using the experience and success of other teachers as encouragement.'

If teachers are to reach the point where they feel confident enough not only to experiment but also to face failure and learn from it, then it is essential that the initial floundering that is a part of any challenge is not smoothed over in an attempt to 'help'. The ability to face and use classroom dilemmas productively should be highly valued as an objective. It is vital that appropriate support be available to teachers so that the element of challenge does not become destructive. Strategies for this kind of support are outlined later in this chapter.

2 Working in isolation inhibits sustained change

The most effective support comes from other teachers who are having similar experiences.

> 'I need to feel that other teachers are suffering from the same pressures as myself. It is useful simply to be able to talk, exchange ideas and renew enthusiasm which inevitably wanes when you feel you are on your own. Whether they succeeded or failed, such experiences are useful in forming one's own "plan of attack".'

Changes in approach have been best stimulated when groups of teachers have come together to share ideas, compare classroom strategies and engage in some mathematics. Colleagues discussing and working together on common problems has helped not only to remove the feeling of isolation but also to promote greater insight into pupils' learning of mathematics. The value of shared experiences has been evident also where teachers have begun to work with each other in their classrooms. Cooperative teaching has often proved a particularly powerful stimulus for facilitating change. One teacher wrote:

> 'All too often people will look at pupils' work from other teachers and conclude "Mine could never do that." This cooperative teaching has been an opportunity for teachers to see their own pupils not only enjoying and getting involved with their mathematics but also producing work that they never though they could. This is, to my mind, the most significant spur for change anyone could have.'

3 Teachers must evolve their own strategies for successful action in their individual classrooms

When teachers face difficulties, or are searching for new strategies, they often look for and are given 'solutions' by advisory staff, lecturers and others who are deemed 'expert'. These agencies must act as catalysts in order to stimulate and facilitate professional development. It is only when teachers are given time to reflect on their experiences and come up with their own solutions and strategies that change becomes lasting and self-sustained. Teachers are often not given credit for the personal resources they have, and therefore undervalue their own experiences.

STATEMENT 13
The recognition that expertise lies in teachers' own experiences is fundamental to the developmental process.

The following is an extract from an account of an in-service course:

'Teachers arrived for their second session, having tried out some mathematical activities with their classes that they had worked on together at the previous session some weeks before. After discussing their classroom trials, they generated a list of problems and then began to pool suggestions for "solving" the problems they had raised. It is interesting that some suggestions were seemingly contradictory, but it became clear to the group that the exercise was not about finding the answer, but about pooling experiences and hence increasing their range of classroom strategies. The following are a selection of their problems and "solutions":

1 Practical activities are considered "babyish" by pupils, parents and other teachers. What do I do about this?

   First of all, are *you* convinced that they are not "babyish'"? Second, are you convinced that these activities are mathematical? If not, do some for yourself with your colleagues and talk about them. Try offering the activities to "bright" pupils. Try talking to your pupils about your experiences of working on these activities with other adults and older/brighter pupils. This gives them credibility and status. Try showing textbooks and exam papers to confirm to the pupils that the activities they do are "respectable". If as a result of the activity they can be shown that they can then do "Exercise C", you are on to a winner.

2 Investigative and practical work might not allow pupils to improve their score on tests nor their performance in exams. Should I carry on regardless?

   Try and see. Often the key to success in any test is confidence. If the activity you offer increases pupils' confidence, it can only help. If what you offer and what you test are very different, do question the effectiveness of your tests as well. The GCSE exam requires pupils to engage in practical, investigative and oral work.

3 Pupils may have done the problem but be unable to verbalize their processes. How can I help?

   Are you sure they can't verbalize? They might be used to a right/wrong answer atmosphere and might lack the confidence to offer explanations in other contexts. It takes a long time for pupils to trust you when you invite *their* views, and often they feel they still have to play "guess what's in teacher's mind" games. If pupils have succeeded at a task and enjoyed it, they will want to share it with others and talk about it. Engineer situations which will allow them to do this. That might often mean leaving them to talk with other pupils.'

4 All teachers must be involved in jointly developing schemes of work, assessment models and so on

A visitor to a weekend conference wrote:

'It gave me insight into a way of teachers working together, an in-service model I have never heard of let alone experienced before. A common view is that teachers have little to offer but much to learn. I have seen that if someone is valued and given credibility they are then able to offer a great deal. This takes longer than arranging a "tutor-directed" in-service course but is probably more effective.'

Efforts to improve mathematics teaching often centre on giving teachers 'props' to help them understand and carry out innovations. These may take the form of checklists, simple guidelines, external assessment models, schemes or organizational systems. These stand little chance of succeeding if teachers are not involved in either their evolution or working at the implications affecting their own situation. Strategic expertise from facilitators is essential in capitalizing on teachers' strengths and hence lead to productive outcomes.

5 Effective change will take time and effort – there are no short cuts

Often 'props' are given to teachers with the expectation that this will speed up the developmental process. As sustained change can only come about through a change in teachers' attitudes, this is likely to prevent effective teacher development. Time must be allowed for teachers to become fully involved as it is their professional responsibility to keep up to date through continuing professional development. The close examination on one's professional performance needs commitment and time for reflection, discussion and building of confidence. No matter how attractive it may seem, smoothing over these difficulties in the hope of achieving more rapid success is futile.

> STATEMENT 14
> If sustained change is to be effected, it is necessary to explore ways of making time available for teachers to work together as part of a regular pattern of in-service provision. However, to provide time without paying adequate attention to the quality of the in-service experience is of little value.

In all the above five points, there are clear parallels between learning activities for children and in-service provision for teachers. Pupils need time for discussion and time for reflection. They need to take responsibility for their own learning and for developing their own strategies. They require challenge and need to be able to make mistakes and to go down blind alleys without feeling a failure. Their mathematical development follows no predetermined regular pattern, and they are capable of becoming far more confident and effective in the subject. These parallels can easily be overlooked by in-service providers.

As teachers are usually successful individuals who have had little experience of academic difficulty, they may understand pupils' feelings and difficulties better when they have been through a similar experience themselves. A teacher on a diploma course commented:

'I was surrounded by more able mathematicians and I knew that some of the tutors were aware of the initial problems I was experiencing. However, during the second term the situation began to improve and I settled down and grew in confidence. I must say that this experience in itself has been invaluable as a teacher. I have become much more aware and sympathetic to problems having experienced the feelings of inadequacy myself.'

This has implications for all those involved in educational provision whatever their function. Everyone can benefit from the direct experience of being in a learning situation.

If teachers are to become more confident and effective in the classroom by the means indicated in this chapter, then it is essential that in-service providers believe that teachers are capable of developing their own strategies and evaluating their own and their pupils' work. In the same way that teachers' dominant beliefs determine their behaviour, beliefs about the capabilities of teachers directly determine the mode of, and provision for, in-service work. For example, if in-service providers believe that it is only 'exceptional' teachers who can manage without 'props', then they will not put teachers they consider 'ordinary' into the position where they have to devise their own strategies. A teacher-researcher wrote:

'Having worked regularly with a group of teachers over a period of a few months, I was surprised and a little worried to have what I was doing in my school dismissed on the grounds that I was a "special" teacher, and that "ordinary" teachers would not be able to cope with or effect such change.

I reflected on this accusation, and came to the conclusion that the only thing that was special about me was the fact that I had had the opportunity and time to work with other teachers on practical classroom issues. Through this involvement we have all become more honest and articulate about our successes and failures, and it appears we are now deemed "special".

It amused and worried me that this incident has a direct parallel with those teachers who dismiss successful work done by pupils in bottom sets by claiming "My low attainers are worse than your low attainers." '

If in-service providers are inhibiting teacher development by providing 'props' and 'solutions', then how can they and others play a facilitating role? Some strategies which prove successful are listed below:

- Enabling contacts to be made between teachers from different schools, groups and local authorities.

- Acting as catalysts in order to ensure that professional development of the kind indicated in this chapter is stimulated, supported and sustained.

- Helping teachers to set up their own groups and aiding in the administration.

- Using advisory teams in a fully supportive role. Imposing them as 'model' demonstration teachers has proved unhelpful and often counter-productive.

- Facilitating collaborative teaching and curriculum development generally, on a regular basis through imaginative and flexible timetabling.

- Recognizing the need for teachers to be allowed time to experiment with ideas obtained on courses. Putting pressure on these teachers to report back too early in an official capacity or present them as 'expert' has been counter-productive.

- Achieving teacher release through extra staffing and ensuring continuity is provided for the pupils. This is best done by incorporating these extra teachers into the staffing of a school rather than employing them on an occasional ad hoc basis.

SUMMARY

The Situation

- Good teachers are education's best resource and are capable of becoming more confident and effective in the classroom, with appropriate challenge and support.

- If teachers are not given credit for the personal resources they have, they will tend to undervalue their own experiences and expertise.

- Convictions shape consistent behaviour. If attempts to bring about change rely solely on changing schemes or examinations, then even though the material teachers use in the classroom may be different, their approach to mathematics teaching and learning will remain essentially the same.

- For many, teaching is an isolating job and working in isolation inhibits sustained change.

- 'Props' such as checklists, simple guidelines, external assessment models, schemes and organizational systems, though well intentioned, are likely to inhibit teacher development.

Recommendations

- Effective change will take time and effort. Ways of making time available for teachers to work together need to be explored as part of a regular pattern of in-service provision. However, to provide time without paying adequate attention to the quality of the in-service experience is of no value.

- In-service providers must act as 'catalysts' in order to ensure that regular professional development is stimulated and facilitated. Teachers must be actively involved in this process in order to develop their confidence, motivation, autonomy and professionalism both in providing for their pupils' needs and in terms of their own mathematics.

- Professional development must be recognized as a long-term and continuous process. Short cuts are a false economy.

- If changes in teachers' behaviour are to be facilitated, teachers must be involved in challenging and critically examining their own beliefs so that they can assume professional responsibility.

- In-service providers must believe that teachers are capable of developing in the ways we have indicated. Hence, they too must be involved in challenging and critically examining their own beliefs.

- In-service providers must not be tempted to smooth over the uncertainties and challenges that are an inherent and essential part of teacher development. The ability to face and use dilemmas productively should be highly valued as an objective.

Chapter 5

Widespread, sustained curriculum development

A teacher wrote:

'The project I was involved with was envisaged as a teacher supportive, unit-based primary scheme conceived in response to criticisms at that time. Its philosophical and organizational basis was exhaustively constructed by a group of practising teachers.

I was involved from the start, making new friends in local schools and meeting the advisory staff at my own and at others' schools. A support group had been formed and trial schools, of which we were one, had a commitment to feed back comments and results to the teacher-writers, either personally or through the advisory team.

It worked well to start with – teachers were less reticent than usual about their experiences, and wrote copiously in order that the units could be improved.

However, under pressures from the publishers, the county advisory staff now changed their attitude to in-service provision, their position on who should write the material, what sort of trials it should receive and even the format of the finished material. The pressure to publish forced them to short-circuit the patterns of development outlined above.

The rush to print led them to produce more and more material themselves, or to commission it from college personnel or from the new advisory teachers or from secondary teachers, for use in the primary sector.

The feedback sessions fell into acrimony, the number of courses led by teachers diminished, the coordinators' courses were cancelled and problems that teachers said they were having with the material were treated as attacks on the scheme itself. The scheme was seen as a monolithic structure, providing all that a child's development required. "Ordinary' teachers" responses and suggestions were ignored.'

This chapter is concerned with curriculum development that aims to improve action in the classroom on a widespread and sustained basis. Involvement in such curriculum development is at present not accepted as part of every teacher's responsibility. Although it is considered acceptable and even expected that teachers should evaluate, assess and amend organizational structures such as schemes, setting or mixed ability, they are often not considered by themselves or others to be capable of acting as authorities on the fundamental issue of children's learning. It is indicative of this situation that practising teachers do not often read educational journals or research findings, seeing in them little relevance to their own experiences. There needs to be recognition that involvement in curriculum development and research are essential parts of the teacher's role.

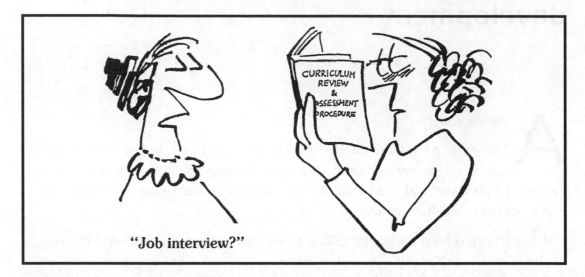

Figure 5.1

STATEMENT 15
Teaching is a researching activity. It is not desirable to disconnect the two functions. Isolation and detachment have their place in the type of enquiry that aims to accumulate knowledge. However, if the enquiry aims to improve action in the mathematics classroom, then such isolation and detachment will bring failure.

We have identified that where initially successful curriculum development has failed to become widespread, it is because of a 'detachment' – a cut off from the original source of inspiration. Section A of this chapter concerns the reasons why detachment occurs and Section B outlines some strategies for avoiding such detachment.

SECTION A: Reasons for detachment

1 Where the curriculum developers/theorists/researchers are detached from the classroom

In some cases, development aimed at improving actions in classrooms seem doomed from the outset when those involved have never been in classrooms themselves. This lack of direct experience from teachers' problems can lead to efforts being misdirected in the first place.

In other cases, it is classroom teachers who are removed, and often promoted, in order to engage in curriculum development. Even with direct classroom experience behind them, this detachment can lead to problems. There is a danger of their perceptions about the job of teaching becoming 'romanticized'. Memories of day-to-day pressures of school life such as writing reports or difficult classes are not as sharp, even after a short period of absence.

This problem is evident even with respect to in-service models. A university lecturer who for four years had run a professional in-service diploma course for experienced teachers was concerned about the effectiveness of a full-time one-term release pattern as compared to a one-day-a-week release model:

> 'Although on the one-term course there are advantages for teachers in not having to worry about the school organization and hence immerse themselves in the course, there were a number of difficulties. It was easy to forget some of the circumstances in which the classroom problems occurred, and hence the solutions teachers found to these problems on the course were not always effective. There were also problems about "rehabilitation" after the term's absence.

> The one-day-a-week model, with two one-week residential elements, fulfils more effectively the main aim of the course in enabling teachers to develop and improve their craft of teaching. This is because they can teach and reflect at the same time. The opportunities for trying out ideas in the classroom, observing and discussing these with other teachers, modifying approaches and then re-testing them regularly, enables growth of confidence, awareness and competence. With the one-day-a-week model this "active reflection" becomes so much a part of a teacher's practice, that there is a greater chance of it continuing after the end of the course on a sustained basis, especially when local support groups play a role.

> This model also has the advantage of allowing teachers to work and communicate with their school colleagues without developing a detached language or status. On the full-time course this is not always possible and it causes some of the rehabilitation problems mentioned above. I have also noticed that the one-day-a-week course leads to much greater departmental involvement in teachers' schools.'

STATEMENT 16
Where research is embedded in teachers' own experience it holds more meaning and credibility for them.

There is also a danger of a cultural gap developing between practising teachers and those who have taken on curriculum development posts. Teachers often become suspicious and cynical about these new 'experts' as it is seen as a way out from the drudgery of working with 'real things', a way to attain status, more money and better working conditions. These aspects often detract from the educational value of a development.

Where any group or individual is involved in a curriculum development project there is always the danger of a 'club' mentality forming. An 'in-language' and complacency can set in, leading to an inability and even an unwillingness to communicate with anyone else, or on anything but their own terms. It is essential that communication is two-way and is based on the sharing of common experiences.

> ## STATEMENT 17
> If curriculum change is to be widespread and sustained, it is essential that developments do not remain focused around a small group of apparently successful and enthusiastic individuals.

2 Where the curriculum development begins in the classroom with practising teachers but becomes detached in the dissemination process

A head of department wrote:

'I find it frustrating when I come across a number of teaching projects in final boxed forms without any indication of the thinking, experimenting, selecting, trials and testing which went on during the writing of these projects.

Another thing that worries me about these teaching projects is that most have been written as short-term remedies and yet they seem to be presented and used as if they are there to survive forever.

What should be built into projects, either to equip them for long-term survival or to point out their short-term nature? The latter would be difficult to achieve because vast resources are invested in many projects and regarding them as short-term would not justify these investments.'

It is often the case that curriculum development projects are conceived in order to tackle specific problems such as mixed-ability groupings, investigational and practical activities, coherence or individualized work. These are usually carried out by groups of interested, committed and enthusiastic teachers. The development involves these teachers in discussion, reflection, classroom experimentation, evaluation and modification. This personal involvement almost invariably leads to successful outcomes in terms of pupils' motivation, enjoyment and attainment. The problems begin with the attempt to achieve widespread dissemination. It is quite natural that these groups of individuals wish to share their success with others. Invariably, though, it is the 'end point' that the group disseminates. In reality, the success of their ventures depended upon their personal active engagement. The material is emphasized rather than the experience.

In-service work associated with widespread dissemination frequently focuses only on clear explanations of how to use material. Whereas such developments might be locally successful in well motivated departments, these stand little chance of achieving national curriculum change because they become detached from the original source of inspiration.

External pressures from publishers, local authorities and central government can contribute to the feeling that the end point or product is more important than the developmental aspects of a project. The offer of publication can be seductive to teachers, but the involvement of these external agencies can often dictate the pace, nature and integrity of a development, as is illustrated by the teacher writing at the beginning of this chapter.

This change of emphasis becomes even more exaggerated when the materials become a commercial success. A teacher concerned about the apparently unforeseen effects of such developments wrote:

> 'In the late 1950s, a similar climate existed in maths education to that which we now experience. There was a strong pressure for change in maths curricula from the OEEC (Organisation for European Economic Cooperation) through the Royaumont Conference of 1959 and within England from pressure groups.
>
> They pushed for change – talked about much the same things which we want now – and published texts. For the people involved in the preparation of these texts – SMP, MME, St Dunstan's and so on – the process was lengthy and laborious and involved major changes in things other than content.
>
> However, these texts were seized on as a quick way to get "up to date" and to change what existed in many schools. If you taught from the texts, you must be okay. Change could be implemented easily by learning a few new tricks yourself (sets, matrices, transformations) and then teaching them in the same old way. Apparently, quick and easy solutions are not going to work.'

Failure to invest in a more complete involvement of teachers can give rise to the myth that not all teachers are capable of understanding the rationale and philosophy behind a development. Further, this lack of involvement can lead to the outright rejection of materials by teachers or to its misuse.

STATEMENT 18
No imported curriculum development exercise can be effective without working commitment and teacher involvement.

Our own experience has shown us the consequence of people taking on material in good faith, not having had sufficient personal involvement in its development or use. For example, an eager advisory teacher concerned to disseminate what she saw as excellent LAMP Project ideas took some draft in-service material, reproduced it in reduced form and prepared to send it out to all schools in the area. The material was designed to be used in an interactive manner to stimulate and focus discussion and classroom experimentation. The advisory teacher seemed surprised that the material was badly received!

The detachment of teachers from the original aims and purposes of a development can lead them to take up only its more obvious aspects. In this way, a teaching system, scheme of workcards, booklets or textbooks can become an end in itself. This account is from a teacher who visited a school that used such a system:

'In every classroom I went into, the style of pupil working and the attitudes of pupils and staff to the mathematics going on was similar. The pupils worked on their own, and even the Year 7 were familiar with their system. Comments took the form:

"Who's got the answer book?"
"Oh, I did that card last week, the answer's …"
"Who's got card no …?"
"How many more have you got to do before you finish your matrix?"
"Aren't you on the test yet?"
"Sir, have you worked out my next matrix?"

I asked many pupils what they thought of the work, but only got comments about the scheme and its organization:

"I like getting on to the next card."
"It would be better if there were more answer books."

I tried to focus more on the mathematics by asking them to talk about what they were doing. In general, they spoke without much confidence or conviction. A few did seem intrigued by some aspect of their work, but when I tried to provoke them into asking their own questions about it, they politely said they would prefer just to finish it so that they could tick it off and get on to the next card.

The teachers explained their role – they had to decide which cards a pupil should do next helped by a vast network provided for them by the scheme, and of course help when the pupils are stuck. They explained that even though the system is hard to set up, once there it made their life a lot easier.

I left the school depressed and sat down to analyse why. It came down to the fact that I had seen little mathematics. The pupils rarely worked in groups and therefore had no real opportunity to talk to each other about their work. Even the discussions I had had with pupils and staff had focused almost entirely around "the system". Although many of the pupils were enjoying their work and were secure about where they were in the scheme, and although the teachers were secure and comfortable too, the mathematical activity going on in the classrooms seemed superficial.

I began to think about those who had been involved at first hand in creating the scheme. I was sure that their classrooms would be different. What was it that had happened or not happened in the transfer?

I still like the material, I still like some of the philosophy, and I am sure that my "snapshot" view of the system at work may not be representative. I am also sure, however, that I had seen an organization that had in some respects "taken over" and had left pupils with a view of mathematics where the important thing was to get onto the next card and which prompted them when asked what they did yesterday to reply "Card H.45".'

SECTION B: Avoiding detachment

Within the six local authorities involved with LAMP, we saw the power of teacher support groups as well as more specific 'task'-oriented teacher working groups concerned with issues such as assessment, parents and industry. These groups were all very different. They started up in a variety of ways, their meetings had different formats, they had different emphases and they gave rise to other groups.

> **STATEMENT 19**
> To succeed on a wider scale, dissemination must be firmly rooted in the personal experiences of teachers in their classrooms. Hence it must depend on personal contact based on shared experience. This can only be achieved through involving more and more teachers in active support networks.

The LAMP network groups were not isolated. The focus provided by the project enabled connections to be made between the various groups. They drew and fed from each other, and together they formed a powerful and growing support network. The fact that the groups once initiated have been largely self-sustaining, have flourished and continued to grow throughout the period of the project (1983–86) illustrates the importance attached to them by teachers. Attempts to generate such a network for teachers by imposing a structure of formally constituted groups is unlikely to succeed, as this support group member indicates:

> 'The formalities and career-linked high profile leadership of imposed groups would be totally different in character to the informality and low profile "leadership" of the original teacher-initiated groups. Moves from the top may lead to those groups being formally set up by LAs or others with the result that the original groups disappear.'

The organic nature of the project network ensured that the type of detachment described earlier could not easily occur. Its growth depended on the teachers within it. They wanted to share their successes, but were not disseminating a set of materials, or even a set of ideas. They were, instead, involving more teachers in working together to enable them to develop their own strategies and hence become more confident and competent in their classrooms. Dissemination of this kind is not easy or quick, but it is effective and long lasting because it is firmly rooted in the personal experiences of teachers in their classrooms. Teachers do not view their development as 'a fad' that will disappear along with all the others because their beliefs about learning and mathematics have changed.

A project coordinator wrote:

'For the project, teachers are an integral part of the research and development process. By necessity this involves them in examining critically their beliefs and practices and comparing their findings with previous research and curriculum development studies. Both as researchers and as critics of other research their ability to facilitate their colleagues' development and enhance the quality of pupils' learning is increased considerably.

The current phase of the project includes cluster groups of teachers working on areas of common interest based on the competencies – mental methods, special needs, progression from primary to secondary phases, problem solving, mathematics language, questioning techniques, teaching approaches, calculators and calculating, life skills and opportunities for developing numeracy outside the classroom. At one level, the teachers are addressing day-to-day classroom needs through working on these areas but at another level, these very pragmatic activities are acting as a catalyst for the teachers to develop greater insight into the role of the competencies as an aid to improving pupils' mathematical understanding.

The extent to which teachers became engaged in the project is as complex as the project's focus. For example, involvement has led some teachers to undertake research degrees to explore some of the issues in considerable depth. Many teachers, as a result of the project, have registered for postgraduate qualifications as a means of offering a focus and discipline for their work. For some, the project remains a means of improving classroom practice.

There are two aspects of this which need further study:

1 The ebb and flow of teachers' energies and engagement.

2 The trigger points which lead teachers to pursue in-depth classroom research.'

SUMMARY

The Situation

- Participation in curriculum development and research are not seen as integral parts of the job of teaching.

- Teachers are often not considered by themselves or others to be capable of acting as authorities on the matter of children's learning.

- Where initially successful curriculum development has failed to become widespread, it is because of a 'detachment' – a cut-off from the original source of inspiration.

- The most important part of any curriculum development is teacher involvement. This has invariably led to dissemination of a written product only. External pressures have often dictated the pace, nature and integrity of the development.

- The focus provided by the project has facilitated:

  a) the formation of various working groups of teachers

  b) the continuation of groups after the completion of their initial task or course

  c) connections between the various groups hence maximizing their impact.

Recommendations

- There needs to be recognition that participation in curriculum development and research are essential parts of the teacher's role and responsibility.

- In order to achieve widespread, successful and sustained curriculum development, teachers must be allowed time and organizational support.

- If curriculum change is to be widespread and sustained, it is essential that developments do not remain focused around a small group of apparently successful and enthusiastic individuals.

- To succeed on a wider scale, dissemination must be firmly rooted in the personal experiences of teachers in their classrooms. It must depend upon a cellular growth of working groups based on personal contact. This can be achieved only through involving more and more teachers in active support networks.

Chapter 6

Schemes

This chapter is concerned with published schemes, home-made schemes and the use of resources.

SECTION A: Published schemes

We have found cause for concern in the adverse effects that a close adherence to a published scheme can have on both children's learning of mathematics and teachers' professional development. Seven of these concerns are outlined below.

Concern 1

Investigatory or enquiry elements of schemes are often left out by teachers, frequently because of 'syllabus pressures'. This is an age-old problem. In trying to resolve this, some schemes have attempted to include enquiry as a compulsory component of their course. However, there are two problems with this.

1. Because the more stretching investigatory elements of some schemes are not reached until initial material has been completed by pupils, it is often only the quicker children who get a taste of this kind of work. All children need and benefit from mathematical exploration.

2. When given greater status, and often in order to 'help' the teacher, investigatory elements can become prescriptive and limiting, precluding the teachers' and children's own questions and losing all sense of real enquiry or exploration. The following writing illustrates this concern:

   'Why is it that some schemes offer an "Investigations" chapter or booklet? All too often these consist of a long list of questions beautifully annotated and carefully structured so ensuring that pupils will be able to work independently and have enough to get on with, but offer no encouragement to ask questions of their own.

   If all the questions come from text and worksheets or are asked by me, then what is the essence within the mathematical experience undergone by my pupils that warrants my calling it an investigation?

   The word is becoming devalued – perhaps we should avoid it.'

Concern 2

New schemes are often chosen because they are seen to cater for a particular organizational classroom priority. However, the 'prices' that are paid for these priorities may well have adverse effects on the children's mathematical experiences. For example, if the priority is to ensure that pupils can 'get on' independently of their teacher, there is a danger that a scheme which provides for this may also lead to the mathematical content being unnaturally fragmented.

Concern 3

By their nature, most schemes are answer-oriented, some to make life easier for teachers, some to encourage pupils to 'work back' from solutions and some to enable pupils to mark their own work so as not to hamper their speed of progression. One teacher writes of the answer-oriented view his scheme has given his pupils:

> 'As work is self-marked, only questions with a single answer are asked … but some of the cards do say "What do you notice?" Pupils quickly learn that there is *an* answer to this too and either look up answers or ask a teacher, who provides the words.

> Responses not in the exact form of words in the answer sheets are marked wrong by pupils. Any teacher intervention in this process, with positive encouragement to speculate, is viewed with suspicion. Authority rests with the answer sheets!'

Concern 4

Many mathematics schemes now include computer software packages. There is, however, a danger that computers may not realize their potential as powerful vehicles for mathematical enquiry and development in the classroom. Although many of the programs within the packages can provide excellent starting-points for exploration, some are no more than simulations of what are considered to be successful classroom activities. When these activities are 'translated' for us on a computer, they sometimes lack flexibility, precluding and limiting opportunities for pupils to follow up their own ideas or organize their own work. All too often the packages in general are used as 'rewards' and devices to 'keep the pupils occupied'.

Concern 5

The teacher's role can be undermined by a close adherence to a polished scheme. A teacher wrote:

> 'My horror stories are not so much the schemes as the teachers who:
> - go in knowing that 25 March means p. 47 Book 2
> - rely on their scheme to prepare their lessons for them
> - feel that published schemes know better than they do
> - are so bound by the structure of a scheme that they can't, or don't want to try anything else

- think it's the scheme's and examination's job to motivate their pupils

- feel too uncomfortable to be open minded about change.'

Much of the undermining occurs because a scheme is seen to take over classroom responsibilities that should be those of the teacher. Responding to the immediate needs of individual children, controlling material, deciding what should happen next and what pathways of learning should be encouraged are all essential parts of the teacher's role and cannot be generalized by an external system written for unknown children and teachers. Expecting published material to give this kind of support, is asking for something that cannot be provided externally.

Concern 6

Frequently, an adherence to a scheme is seen as a necessary support for so-called 'weak teachers'. However, even as a short-term solution this can be unsatisfactory and often counter-productive. This is also true of the understandable concern expressed about newly qualified teachers of mathematics as this head of department indicates:

> 'If, as I believe, teaching is improved through reflecting on our classroom experiences, then to consider a scheme as something that will "make it okay" for an NQT is arrant nonsense, since it denies the ways in which teachers develop their abilities.

> Most schemes, by appearing to make an NQT an effective teacher – that is, able to keep the class "happy" and "occupied at their tasks" – can undermine that teacher's development, hiding the real need for it.

> Schemes need to be "patchy" in order that the teacher has to take responsibility for the development in children of the processes and strategies of mathematical activity.'

For all teachers, support and development of the kind indicated throughout this report are essential.

A considerable part of the teaching of mathematics is carried out by non-specialists. These are sometimes strong teachers of their first subject, and it is commonly assumed that they will benefit from even more guidelines and will need a strictly prescriptive mathematics scheme. We have found, however, that the development of these teachers is also undermined by such a provision. When allowed the time for an element of 'retraining', their development is also facilitated and they can become significant members of a mathematics department, bringing unique insights and making valuable contributions. A tutor on such a retraining course wrote:

> 'It was interested to see that teachers arrived with a very limited idea of mathematics and mathematics teaching.

> Having been given the opportunity on the course to engage in mathematics themselves in an exploratory and creative way, and thus experience the positive aspects of the subject, they began to realize their own capabilities in mathematics.

This experience also enabled them to see how successful teaching approaches from their own subject area could be used in this new area of the curriculum.

One teacher told me about how she taught English, describing how she collected materials, utilized the pupils' own ideas and generally fuelled their creativity. The realization slowly dawned on her that she could teach mathematics in the same way.'

> ### STATEMENT 20
> Schemes are offered in good faith by advisers, headteachers and other concerned agencies to teachers of mathematics as 'solutions' to classroom problems. In practice, strict adherence to these schemes fundamentally undermines the principles of teacher development, and can become major inhibitors to improvement in the quality of mathematics teaching.

Concern 7

New schemes are often taken on in order to initiate change in static teaching situations dominated by exposition and textbooks. Sometimes this is in order to respond to national initiatives. We have found that where a department is aware that the new scheme is merely a starting-point for discussion and development it has been beneficial. However, in many cases, even when schemes have been taken on in this spirit, they have failed to facilitate development for a range of understandable reasons: key teachers may leave; financial investment inhibits rejection or updating; and busy teachers with other responsibilities who would have been in a strong position to contribute to departmental development become reluctant to endanger what is for them a familiar, administratively efficient system. In these all too frequent cases, the scheme becomes a substitute for genuine teacher development rather than a vehicle for it, and the quality of the children's mathematics learning may well not be improved. Teachers begin to teach 'the scheme' rather than teach mathematics.

> ### STATEMENT 21
> No mathematics scheme alone can meet the needs of pupils. The mathematical development of pupils can only be encouraged, sustained, evaluated and assessed by the personal involvement of their teachers. It is not possible to produce a definitive scheme that will apply to all pupils or situations, even within specific ability ranges.

SECTION B: Home-made schemes

Faced with the above problems, or in efforts to increase departmental involvement, or in order to deal with a school-specific problem (mixed ability, team teaching and so on), many departments decide to produce their own schemes, often based on a prescribed sequence of home-made workcards, booklets or worksheets. We have found that in time there is a real danger of these schemes becoming as habitual as published schemes and that in many cases the same problems are to be found. Added to these is the strength of attachment that is derived from the expenditure of personal time and effort. This makes change and flexibility that much harder to achieve. A head of department wrote:

'Teachers cannot afford to be sentimental about the form of organization, resources, methods and so on when they accept responsibilities for the mathematical growth of their pupils. They need much greater confidence in themselves so that they can "kick around" and experiment with new methods and materials. They need to develop their power to live, change, grow and respond so that they can meet changes and disturbances which are present in life. This they can hardly begin to develop if most of their energies and beliefs are invested in methods, organization and "materials".'

Home-made schemes, and even departmental schemes of work, are often designed to be as flexible as possible, but without continual re-evaluation and modification involving the whole department, a scheme can quickly stagnate and its content take on a higher significance than was meant. A teacher wrote:

'I'm really concerned about the power of the written word. Once something has been formalized it can take on a far greater importance than was perhaps originally intended.

Last summer two teachers put together a Year 9 scheme of work – some of it based upon what they had done with their own groups over the year. It meant very little to me when I first read it. I didn't understand why it was organized the way it was, why the content included particular topics and not others, or why the activities listed had been chosen.

The entire document seemed useless to me. I abandoned it, along with several other teachers in the department, and instead we got together and tried to sort out what we were going to do about it.

On reflection, if I'd been involved in the formation of the departmental scheme of work, I'd have realized the flexibility that was implicit in its structure.'

STATEMENT 22
A scheme cannot be a substitute for an ongoing dialogue with colleagues. This generates more ideas and an increased awareness of pupils' needs. The continuing process of development is more important than the particular details of the curriculum. There are no short cuts and the process takes time.

SECTION C: Using resources

Good resources can be used well.
Good resources can be used badly.
Bad resources can be used well.
Bad resources can be used badly.

A teacher described an incident with a bottom set, Year 8 class:

'Two girls came up to me and asked if they could do some "sums". They were fed up with what they were doing. I had some very old textbooks in a cupboard that were full of exercises containing dozens of "sums" ranging from the four rules to quadratic equations. They were meant as practice for pupils of considerably higher age and ability than these girls, but I rather dismissively told them they could choose something from them to do if they wanted.

When I got back to them they were happily engaged in experimenting with their calculators in order to obtain answers to an exercise entitled "Changing Vulgar Fractions into Decimals".

Not only were they not put off by the title but the only piece of sound knowledge they had was that a half equals 0.5. From this piece of information they were successfully completing the exercise.'

Pupils in this class were used to asking their own questions about their mathematics and hence when offered material that would seem to be extremely uninviting, they accepted it, as they normally would, as a challenge. Their personal motivation was sufficient for them to sustain exploration on their own and achieve good results.

> **STATEMENT 23**
> When teachers and pupils are accustomed to exploring mathematical ideas and have established a positive attitude to learning, then almost any material can be used as a stimulus for mathematical enquiry in the classroom.

There is, at present, a wide variety of useful resources available for teachers and pupils in mathematics lessons. These include ideas within existing schemes and textbooks, resources in the form of thematic and topic booklets, books and periodicals containing ideas and 'starters', catalogues and timetables, reference material, magazine and newspaper articles, games and practical materials including calculators and computers, as well as the resources that the children bring with them to school in terms of ideas, interests and miscellaneous items. This has implications in terms of teacher awareness about what is potentially useful in their mathematics classroom and about what physical accommodation is necessary in order to work at the subject effectively. In the first case, we have found that when given the opportunities for teacher development, teachers have become more discerning and more demanding consumers of published material and equipment. In the second, it is essential that senior management do not look upon mathematics as a subject that can be taught in any room in the school.

> **STATEMENT 24**
> It is part of the professional concern of all teachers to take responsibility for choosing appropriate materials and environments that will encourage pupils to learn mathematics. It is this professional responsibility that needs encouragement, time and resources to develop.

SUMMARY

The Situation

- There is cause for concern about the adverse effects that a close adherence to a published scheme can have on children's learning of mathematics.

- Investigatory or enquiry elements of schemes are often left out by teachers, frequently because of 'syllabus pressures'.

- It is often only the quicker children who get a taste of the more stretching investigatory elements of some schemes, because they are not reached until initial material has been completed.

- In many schemes investigatory elements have become prescriptive and limiting.

- By their nature most schemes are answer-oriented.

- Schemes are offered in good faith by advisers, headteachers and other concerned agencies to teachers of mathematics as solutions to classroom problems. In practice, schemes can often become major inhibitors to improvements in the quality of mathematics teaching, because ultimately they can undermine the principles of teacher responsibility.

- It is not possible to produce a definitive mathematics scheme that will apply to all pupils or situations, even within specific-ability ranges.

- Home-made schemes, if not constantly reviewed, will suffer from the same problems as published schemes.

- When teachers and pupils are accustomed to exploring mathematical ideas and have established a positive attitude to learning, then almost any material can be used as a stimulus for mathematical enquiry in the classroom.

- When teachers take the opportunity for professional development, they have become more discerning and more demanding consumers of published material and equipment.

Recommendations

- A scheme must not take over teachers' classroom responsibilities such as responding to the immediate needs of individual children, controlling material, deciding what should happen next and what pathways of learning should be encouraged. These responsibilities are those of the teacher.

- Schemes and schemes of work should be continuously evaluated and modified. This process must include the whole department and is more important than the particular details of the curriculum. There are no short cuts and the process takes time.

- Resources in the form of ideas, thematic and topic booklets, catalogues and timetables, books, periodicals, reference material, magazine and newspaper articles, games and practical materials including calculators and computers are needed. The spending of departmental budgets on 'packaged' schemes only should be seriously questioned by schools as this often means that no funds remain for other forms of resources and can lead to inflexibility.

- It is essential that mathematics is recognized as a subject that has special accommodation requirements.

- It must be seen to be part of the professional concern of all teachers to take responsibility for choosing appropriate materials and environments that will encourage pupils to learn mathematics. It is this professional responsibility that needs encouragement.

Chapter 7

Working across the curriculum

A teacher wrote:

'In my early years of teaching, I used to teach physics and mathematics, and one year I taught both to the same Year 10 group.

I was aware that the physics department among others used to complain about pupils' inability to manipulate formulae and perform what were regarded as simple and basic mathematical skills in their classes. I had a certain amount of sympathy with these complaints as I too had noticed pupils' inability to apply their mathematics in physics lessons.

The year I was allocated the same group for mathematics and physics I thought I would be in a position to change things for the better since I would be able to use the mathematics lessons to teach pupils exactly what they needed in physics. I did.

To my surprise I still found that what most pupils could do confidently in my maths class, they were not able to transfer into their physics lessons with me during the same week! What was even more sad was the fact that they failed to appreciate the joke when I told them that they must have an awful mathematics teacher!'

This problem of lack of transference between disciplines is as old as subject boundaries themselves. Two of the most common strategies designed to deal with the perceived artificiality of subject divisions and resolve problems of this kind have been of particular concern to us: inter-departmental discussions and meetings, and thematic approaches.

Inter-departmental discussions and meetings

'Do you think you could teach trig before we teach refraction?'

'Do you really not teach pi until Year 9?'

'But we always teach them ratio this way.'

'If they want them to know about it, why don't they teach it to them themselves?'

'The science department say that Year 7 can't read off the scales on their measuring cylinders, so I said we'd do "Reading Graphs" as the first topic of the year.'

Frequently inter-departmental meetings are held as responses to perceived external demands. Terms such as 'cross-curricular links', 'inter-disciplinary enquiry', 'integrated curriculum', 'language across the curriculum', 'mathematics across the curriculum', 'life skills' and 'whole-school policies' sound plausible but are often tackled only at an administrative level, concentrating purely on content overlap. A head of department commented on his experiences:

'One thing that leaves me constantly frustrated and dissatisfied is "cross-curricular" links.

I have read reports and heard advisers, inspectors and others pointing out where links exist with other departments.

I have been involved in meetings where attempts to make the curriculum more "coherent" have taken place. Mostly these have been in the form of each head of department explaining his or her scheme and syllabus to others and ending up with an ordered list of topics which each department should cover in order that pupils can cope with certain ideas and principles in various subjects without having to be taught these several times.

I have also been aware that these decisions, however well implemented, have had little effect on pupils' ability to transfer their skills across, or see links between, other subjects.'

Thematic approaches

The frustration caused by the apparent artificiality of subject divisions have led to some initiatives abandoning the discipline boundaries completely. Children explore themes such as 'Christmas', 'Water' or 'Railways', or work on community projects. Theoretically, subject content should emerge in context through such projects and therefore help pupils to gain an overview of the curriculum and see the relevance of particular techniques and skills. In practice, however, this does not always happen. Because of concern that pupils should get the required quota of 'geography' or 'science' out of their project, the subject matter can become trivial and contrived, especially as far as mathematics is concerned.

Both in inter-departmental meetings and in 'thematic' projects of the types described, mathematics is usually seen and discussed only as a 'service subject', especially with regard to 'low attainers'. This reinforces many teachers' and pupils' preconceptions about the nature of mathematics. It is precisely these assumptions that must be tackled if any meaningful cross-curricular work involving mathematics is to be developed. If mathematics is only seen as utilitarian or tied to a theme approach, however practically and relevantly based, then when it is offered in its own right, the subject may be regarded as uninteresting and unimportant. A large part of the mathematical development and experience that we have found essential for all pupils will therefore not occur.

A university lecturer wrote:

'Mathematics has a great deal to offer in terms of its potential for creativity, its special use of language and its opportunities for conjecture, proof and modelling.

To reduce the richness the mathematics specialist can offer to merely doing your calculations for you is as absurd as asking the English specialist just to correct your spelling, the geographer to read your map or the PE specialist occasionally to lead a run around the block.'

STATEMENT 25
If pupils of all abilities are to experience the richness of individual subjects and to gain an overview of the subtle inter-relationships and interactions that exist among disciplines, it is essential to maintain both the links and the separation between subjects.

It is not surprising that there are difficulties in achieving these inter-disciplinary relationships when one considers the deep-rooted stereotypes that exist within schools.

A teacher reported:

'As I was passing the boys' changing room, I heard the PE teacher say to some of my mathematics pupils, "If you don't get changed quickly, you'll be back after school and I'll give you some maths to do."'

Overheard in a head of year office:

'Is geography better now you are sitting next to Tracy?'

'Are you finding it hard to get your science homework done?'

'How are you getting on in English?'

'I know you find maths hard but you really will need it.'

'It's nice to see your history marks have gone up.'

STATEMENT 26
Most of the problems encountered in working across the curriculum are due to, and exacerbated by, the enormous lack of awareness that exists in schools about what everyone else is doing, and about the nature of different subjects. This is especially true of mathematics where strange preconceptions are rife.

When teachers become more aware of what is going on in other classrooms, they are more likely to be able to use that understanding to best effect both in their own subject lessons and in any joint subject initiatives. The climate created by such awareness is a prime factor in breaking down children's stereotypes of teachers' specialist roles. This awareness can only be achieved through teachers working together and being interested in children's experiences in other curriculum areas. Cooperation must develop at teacher level. There are numerous opportunities for senior management to play a facilitating role through flexible timetabling and staffing, altered priorities and so on but when initiatives are imposed by management on their staff without those teachers being involved and committed, then such initiatives are unlikely to be sustained.

When new areas are created for pupils to study that attempt to be cross-curricular in nature – for example, 'Life Skills' or Information Communication Technology – there is a danger that without the general awareness described earlier, they will end up being just another subject slot on the timetable. Those who are not involved will often have little idea of what goes on, thus destroying the spirit behind the initiatives.

Forging effective cross-curricular links

A teacher wrote:

> 'It must be possible to peel away the trimmings, that is, different resources and specific subject language, to concentrate on pupil learning, in order that the pupils can recognize common approaches and become more actively involved in the learning process.'

Teachers associated with the project managed to forge strong, regular and fruitful links with other subject areas. Because these were developed at teacher level, the strategies adopted were all very different according to the opportunities that arose within individual schools. A common feature, however, was that all the teachers have recognized the need to open their lessons to other teachers and work together in their classrooms. This is not always easy, as the following teachers indicate:

> 'Changes across the curriculum will only come from a change in teachers' attitudes towards themselves. Will they have the willingness to open up their classroom doors? Will they have the confidence to admit they don't always know the "best" way for children to do things?
>
> I need to open up my teaching space to others, to invite them in at any time – not just to see the "good" lessons, but to witness the failures as well, so that we might discuss approaches and methods as yet unexplored.'

The writing below is from a mathematics teacher who was interested to see whether a teaching approach that gave pupils more responsibility for their own learning could have the same positive effects in another curriculum area:

'A friendly geographer has taken up the invitation to come into my lessons and he enjoyed the way the children were working and was keen for me to come into his geography lessons.

As with the other cross-curricular discussion I had had, it was important to both of us that our cooperation was not at the level of "When do you teach coordinates and scale?" We were sure that the most important common ground was our joint concern over how we could help children to learn, increase their motivation, and generally allow them more control over their work.

I found myself being genuinely excited by the diversity and richness of the pupils' ideas, and discussing our notes at the end of the first lesson made us both realize that the pupils' discussion had touched upon the geography syllabus for the term. We felt we had to find a way of following up the children's questions and ideas and not simply impose our own onto them.

There followed six weeks of the children working on different aspects of the third world and poverty.

The following elements of our geography project stood out for me as being necessary components of any learning/teaching situation, and as such transferable across all subject areas:

Responsibility and challenge – the pupils were pleased to take on the responsibility and challenge of controlling to a great extent what they did and how they did it. It became their work not ours.

Starting from where the pupils are – because they had to make their own decisions about where and how to start, there was no question of "teaching to the middle of the ability range".

Pupils following through and extending their ideas – in the course of their work, many pupils wrote away to various embassies and individuals for information and opinions. The basic ideas were theirs and their satisfaction and pride were evident when they received replies. In this way, the pupils began to realize that they did have it in them to find things out, not only independently of their teachers, but also outside their teachers' knowledge.

Enjoyment – it is an encouraging sign that when these pupils had to choose their options for Year 10, many who had previously not considered taking geography are now doing so. We in maths do not have to face this ultimate consumer test, but it is interesting to consider what would happen if we did.

I think there are direct parallels here for any subject lesson. The atmosphere was identical to that of my mathematics lessons where, for example, pupils may be working on an idea of their own to which they and I have no idea of an outcome but share an excitement for both the process of discovery and the expectation of results, positive or negative.

It would now be impossible for us not to wish to continue looking at our teaching approaches and exploring classroom strategies that facilitate pupils to learn, gain in confidence and motivation, develop their thinking and study skills as well as widening their appreciation of the subject matter in hand.'

The sustained nature of this work is evident from the comment of the geography teacher who wrote some time later:

'The initial point that struck me when we started working together was that any innovation is best done with more than one person. Trying new things by yourself is very difficult, exhausting and disheartening.

My overall feelings about the work we have done can be summed up in my feelings towards the group. When I taught them in Year 8 they were argumentative, restless and lacking in motivation.

This year, although they have remained quite noisy, they have shown much more interest in the subject. I have been pleased to see how the "quietest", "nervous" personalities in the group have gained in confidence.

We obviously do not give pupils enough responsibility and freedom to come up with their own ideas.'

STATEMENT 27
While each subject area makes a unique contribution to the curriculum, all share a common concern for the development of pupils' knowledge, skills and attitudes. Changes in teachers' attitudes to learning have considerable implications for individual classrooms and hence have the potential for development across all subjects.

In Chapter 2, 'Children learning mathematics', we reported on the attempt by a group of teachers to describe the necessary ingredients for a rich mathematical activity. In the light of the preceding teachers' experiences, it is interesting to see how easily one can generalize the list:

What makes a rich mathematical activity?

- It must be accessible to everyone at the start.
- It needs to allow further challenges and be extendable.
- It should invite children to make decisions.
- It should involve children in speculating, hypothesis making and testing, proving and explaining, reflecting, interpreting.
- It should not restrict pupils from searching in other directions.
- It should promote discussion and communication.
- It should encourage originality/invention.
- It should encourage 'what if' and 'what if not' questions.
- It should have an element of surprise.
- It should be enjoyable.

Some teachers were able to obtain release from their normal timetable commitments in order to work in each other's schools, initially in mathematics lessons and then on a broader basis. One teacher writes about the effects of this cooperative work:

'They have introduced a breath of fresh air and enthusiasm – they have opened up a way of promoting communications between different departments. They have made a few of us realize that we are not alone with our ideas and that there are other staff in our school who feel the same way about children and teaching.'

Subsequently this teacher was allowed time to work at building on these links within his own school. We have found that where external funds have been utilized for teacher release, a variety of fruitful initiatives have begun. To be of real value, these initiatives must be based on a strong, shared working commitment.

A mathematics teacher wrote about a different strategy he used to begin to break down preconceptions:

'An English teacher joined me with a class on a day's outing to the West Sussex Institute where she, the pupils and I spent a day doing mathematical activities. She found this particularly useful, not just because of the methods and ideas used, but as an insight into her own reactions to being in a learning situation.'

STATEMENT 28
If sustained, meaningful cross-curricular links are to be effected, then teachers must be provided with mechanisms to work together on a long-term basis.

SUMMARY

The Situation

- Lack of transference between curriculum areas is a common problem.

- Terms such as 'cross-curricular links', 'inter-disciplinary enquiry', 'integrated curriculum', 'language across the curriculum', 'mathematics across the curriculum', 'life skills' and 'whole-school policies' sound plausible but are often only tackled at an administrative level, concentrating purely on content overlap.

- Although well intentioned, 'thematic' projects can suffer from the subject matter becoming trivial and contrived, especially as far as mathematics is concerned.

- Both in inter-departmental meetings and in 'thematic' projects there is a strong danger that mathematics is seen and discussed only as a 'service subject' especially with regard to 'low attainers'.

- Most of the problems encountered in working across the curriculum are due to and exacerbated by the lack of awareness that exists in schools about what everyone else is doing and about the nature of different subjects. This is especially true of mathematics where strange preconceptions are rife.

- While each subject area makes a unique contribution to the curriculum, all share a common concern for the development of pupils' knowledge, skills and attitudes.

Recommendations

- Preconceptions about the nature and difficulty of mathematics must be tackled if any meaningful cross-curricular work involving the subject is to be developed.

- If pupils of all abilities are both to i) experience the richness of individual subjects and ii) gain an overview of the subtle inter-relationships and interactions that exist among disciplines, it is essential to maintain both the links and the separation between subjects.

- Cross-curricular cooperation must be developed at teacher level and be based on a strong, shared working commitment.

- Senior management must play a supportive, facilitating role through, for example, flexible timetabling and staffing.

- If sustained, meaningful cross-curricular links are to be effected, then teachers must be provided with mechanisms to work together on a long-term basis.

Chapter 8

Evaluating and assessing mathematics

A teacher wrote:

'I am involved in instruction and assessment of teachers on a mountain leadership course. Instruction takes place over a number of weekends and assessment takes place in North Wales over the period of a week.

At the end of the week, the dialogue that has taken place continuously with each potential leader is brought to a conclusion. We talk about their leadership, organization, navigation, security on steep ground and so on. If, at the end of the week, assessor and assessed *disagree* about capabilities, then the main aim of the assessment week is not achieved.

Fortunately this rarely happens. Usually teachers leave more confident in some areas and aware of their weaknesses, and how much they should limit their projects. They do so secure in the knowledge that someone with experience agrees with them.

Since the course is part of a national scheme, there are certain obligatory elements. One evening, after spending all day navigating round the mountains, the teachers have to complete a written exam on 'Navigation'. This irritates them, and seems irrelevant. Some consider it insulting. In no case has anyone 'failed' the exam having performed adequately on the mountain. In some cases the reverse has happened!

Perhaps there are some lessons for me to transfer to my mathematics classroom.'

This chapter is concerned with reasons for assessment. It also explores conflicts and contradictions within our system and outlines responsibilities and criteria for evaluating and assessing children's mathematics.

SECTION A: Reasons for assessing

Before we can consider how best to assess and evaluate pupils' mathematics, it is vital to ask why we do it.

Figure 8.1 provides some pupils' perceptions.

> maths exams and assessments
> help you to get used to examinations which
> is very helpful
>
> I think that we are assessed to check
> that we understand what we are being
> taught. It is to make sure we don't just
> listen and then forget about it.
>
> The assessment shows   It judges
> how far we are ahead   pupils and teachers
> of other pupils on   ability to learn
> the same subject   and teach
>
> of ~~proving~~ showing yourself what you have
> learned and what other people's reaction is to
> it is   I also think it is a way

Figure 8.1

There are a number of reasons why we wish to assess our pupils. Some assessment demands originate from perceived external requirements while others are more pupil centred. Six of these reasons are indicated below:

1 Making comparisons

'Pupils like to know where they are?'

Assessment is often about no more than comparisons. Pupils are compared with each other, with a set standard and with themselves. A teacher wrote of his concern:

'Assessment often involves ranking. It sometimes occurs as the end result, but it should not be the sole aim. Assessment should be more about finding out what the child can do. Putting pupils in rank order does not necessarily do this.'

2 Accountability

'I'll give them a test to prove they can do it.'

In answering the question 'Why do we assess our pupils?', a teacher said:

'To justify our teaching methods.'

The education system has always been required to justify itself in terms of 'results'. Thus the publication of examination results in newspapers is seen by some as a way of making public the efficiency of the school and its teachers. A head of department said:

'Why should I change? My examination results are good.'

The kind of justification that emphasizes such results can lead to the achievements and needs of a significant proportion of children ('the bottom 40 per cent') and their teachers being ignored or devalued.

3 Communication

'How's my Tracy getting on then?'

Teachers have a responsibility to communicate to parents and employers about the achievements and difficulties of their pupils. The search for an effective way of fulfilling this need is one in which teachers have been involved for many years. We create 'communication vouchers', that is, examination results, profiles, termly grades and reports, most of which, by their nature, vastly simplify the child's situation in the mathematics classroom and can be misleading. These impoverished 'vouchers' are then used widely by employers and others for selection purposes.

4 Assessment as part of the learning process

An advisory teacher wrote:

'I do not see how one can separate the business of teaching from that of assessing, since they are both going on together for so much of the time in normal classroom practice.

Decisions which we are continually making as we teach – what questions to ask, when to intervene, how to answer – are all based on our assessment of an individual pupil's mathematical development.

Over a period of time, a picture is built up from a larger number of little brush strokes, many of which, as they were made in "live" discussion or activity, are only visible to the teacher.'

> **STATEMENT 29**
> In order to facilitate pupils' mathematical development, assessment must be an integral part of the learning process.

5 Diagnosis

Diagnostic tests have been used for many years in order to ascertain sources of children's difficulties. However, at a national level these tests often provide little information that is useful to the teacher in improving action in the classroom. Internal school tests, though well intentioned, often provide a negative diagnosis and reinforce pupils' failures in a way that can be emotionally distressing.

Figure 8.2 shows what two pupils wrote.

> I felt ill and I didn't want to do it. I thought I would get a very low mark.
>
> before a test I feel nervous
> after a test I feel scared
> because I think that all
> my answers are wrong

Figure 8.2

STATEMENT 30
Helpful diagnostic exploration can only be achieved through a continual dialogue that also identifies and acknowledges positive achievement.

6 Self-evaluation

An advisory teacher wrote:

'... Pupils themselves may know about their own achievement but many will still say, quite wrongly in my opinion, that they are "hopeless at maths" simply because they do not have a good facility with number or have acquired this notion from previous experience.'

It is essential to consider the value of any assessment to the person who is being assessed. Many pupils leave school with an unrealistically low view of their mathematical abilities and potential. Often these views depend upon whether or not they liked their teacher, whether they are male or female, parents' and teachers' perceptions and expectations, or what particular book they were using. Simplistic assessment procedures may exacerbate this situation.

STATEMENT 31
If the assessment process does not allow for pupils to leave school thoroughly versed in self-evaluation, then the assessment process must be considered incomplete.

SECTION B: Incompatibilities

There exists a clear conflict between external and internal motives for assessment. Our system is riddled with incompatibilities, inconsistencies and contradictions as these examples demonstrate:

Employers have more applicants than they can cope with. Decisions still have to be made. When questioned they put great emphasis on qualities such as common sense, flexibility, ability to think and make decisions, and ability to work co-operatively in a team.

When advertised, the main requirements for the job is 'Grade C or above in mathematics'.

What does a grade C tell you about a pupil in this context?

The books are taken in. Sharon has done six pages of work and her teacher takes a long time writing comments and questions in her book before grading it a B.

The books are returned. Sharon quickly flicks through her work and says, 'I got a B'.

Do grades actually stop our pupils evaluating themselves and their work?

Aim: Encourage practical and problem-solving work in the classroom so as to enable pupils to gain experience of using skills flexibly in context.

Assessment: 'Measure and weigh this stick and record your results.'

Teachers, dissatisfied with percentages, grades and rankings, and seeing little communication value coming from 'average 43.22%, 28th out of 34', or even from 'effort B, achievement D', design a leaver's profile which they feel gives a better picture of their pupils' mathematical abilities.

Employers set an entrance test involving complex manipulation of fractions, decimals and imperial/metric conversions.

Investigative work
is important.

Pupils like
investigative work.

We cannot assess it
by timed written
examination.

It is incorporated
into timed tests
and examinations.

Pupils see no
investigative work in
the examination papers.

Pupils are fearful
and stressed by
these examinations.

Investigative work
is not important.

Pupils do not
like investigative
work.

Figure 8.3

STATEMENT 32
If assessment is to be useful and not inhibitive to the pupils, then any assessment structure or process must not be designed principally to meet the needs of any external agency. Effective communication to these external agencies about pupils' mathematical achievements and abilities can only be achieved and developed collaboratively.

SECTION C: Responsibilities for assessment

A head of department wrote:

'A member of my department was off sick and my "free" period that day coincided with a lesson when he would have been taking a Year 8 class. I decided I would use the opportunity to find out some of their views on assessment. I asked them to write down what in their opinion would be the best way (or ways) for me to find out how "good" they are at mathematics.

On reading the replies later, I found the overwhelming majority suggested that:

1 I should ask their teacher

2 I should teach them myself for a week or two.'

Three of the pupils' responses are given in Figure 8.4.

The best possible way of telling how
well we are doing is too ask us
as we are the only ones besides our
teacher that knows.
A test doesn't really tell you how
we are getting on !!!

The best way. is to coming in
to our class and ask us questions, to
come round a talk to us. To help us
then you would know what we do not
know. Also to talk to our teacher.

I don't agree with tests. You are scared and rush your
work. You work better with your friends. I think that a
teacher should sit ain on a lesson, walking around and
looking at peoples works talking to the children and asking
their teacher about their work.

Figure 8.4

It is often held that objectivity is paramount in any assessment, and yet it is self-evident that the people who know most about pupils' mathematical achievements are their teachers. An advisory teacher commented:

'Surely no external testing procedure can be without some of the undesirable side-effects associated with traditional examinations, and, for those who worry excessively about standardization, it needs to be said loud and clear that the results they produced were far from being perfectly reliable; perhaps even more important is that they could only assess a very restricted range of mathematical processes and strategies.

I believe we must work to develop systems in which a large part of any "grade" is a reflection of the very rich assessment picture built up in the course of teaching and that the very essence of such a system must be the enhancement of teachers' sensitivity and confidence in their own assessment, and public recognition and trust of their judgement.'

STATEMENT 33
Teachers are best placed to take responsibility for effectively assessing their own pupils, and they need support in developing appropriate skills.

Many teachers lack the confidence to take on this responsibility. We have found that when teachers have been actively involved in developing and modifying their own assessment procedures in departmental and inter-school groups, they begin to trust their own judgement and realize their own expertise. If teachers are active participants in either the evolution or interpretation of the aims behind assessment systems, there is less likelihood that the initiatives will be looked upon as just another external requirement beyond teachers' control, with the original aims being misrepresented in the classroom.

In order to implement a continuous assessment model that has the pupils' interests as a priority, it is essential to create an atmosphere in the classroom where self-evaluation and dialogue are encouraged. Marking work is regarded as a teacher's duty and an important factor in maintaining standards of work. If, however, it is solely about ticks and crosses, or the aggregation of totals, or superficial comments such as 'Very good', 'A good effort' or 'Merit', then it is difficult to see how it can help foster, in pupils, internal criteria for evaluating their mathematics. On the other hand, when marking is used to encourage a continuing dialogue, with pupils answering teachers' questions and comments, and teachers in turn responding, self-evaluation is nurtured and self-awareness increased. Where assessment schemes are rigid in terms of allocating marks for prescribed outcomes (for example, 4 for 'Generalization', 6 for 'the Conclusion'), they are likely to limit and channel pupils' mathematics as well as inhibit genuine dialogue and self-evaluation.

A working group of teachers, concerned that their assessment and evaluation of their pupils should assist in and be part of the learning process, developed the following criteria for use in their schools.

- Assessment procedures must not dictate what happens in the classroom.

- Any assessment scheme must acknowledge positive achievement.

- Assessment must be a continuing process involving dialogue between pupils/ pupil, teacher/pupil and teacher/teacher.

- All teachers must be involved in the development of their departmental assessment procedures.

- Any assessment structure must be flexible enough to enable pupils to demonstrate their knowledge, understanding and actions in the form considered most appropriate by them and their teacher.

- Any decision made or action taken as a result of an assessment must involve the pupil.

- Assessment should not be seen as being solely in the hands of teachers. Pupils should be encouraged to evaluate and assess their own work.

- The fundamental aim of any assessment should be for the pupils to be able to feel confident about assessing and evaluating themselves.

These proposals have grown out of teachers' experiences in the classroom. If they are to become widespread and be sustained it is essential that the external system, including parents and employers, recognize and support them.

SUMMARY

The Situation

- Teachers are best placed to take responsibility for effectively assessing their own pupils.

- Our present methods for communicating pupils' mathematical achievements to parents, employers and external agencies generally do not provide useful or usable information.

- Diagnostic tests often provide only a negative diagnosis and reinforce pupils' failures in a way that can be emotionally distressing.

- The provision of what are considered to be helpful assessment devices can sometimes override the learning and teaching objectives of pupils and teachers thus harming the assessment process.

Recommendations

- In order to facilitate pupils' mathematical development, assessment must be an integral part of the learning process.

- Helpful diagnostic exploration must be achieved through a continual dialogue that also identifies and acknowledges positive achievement.

- It is essential to consider the value of any assessment to the person who is being assessed. If the process does not allow for pupils to leave school thoroughly versed in self-evaluation, then the assessment process must be considered incomplete. Pupils must be actively encouraged to evaluate and assess their own work.

- If assessment is to be useful and not inhibitive to pupils, then assessment structures or processes must not dictate what is done in the classroom or be designed principally to meet the needs of external agencies.

- Effective communication about pupils' mathematical achievements and abilities must be achieved and developed in collaboration with external agencies.

- If assessment is to be meaningful and support the curriculum, then it is essential that the external system, including parents and employers, recognize and support its value in enhancing learning.

Chapter 9

Parents and carers

Key questions for parents* are:

- What is our education for?

- Who should make the demands?

- Who knows best? The teacher? The child? The parent?

The following remarks were overheard at a mathematics parents' evening:

'My daughter spent hours on her homework doing long division. She was very upset so I tried to help. When I looked, she had got them right, but she was in tears. She didn't understand them.'

'I'm not very good at maths and neither is my daughter.'

'If my teacher hadn't beaten hell out of me and made me do it, I wouldn't be where I am today.'

'I'm worried about the different ways teachers work. They are getting on well with a teacher and are doing well when suddenly they are moved on to the next teacher who has completely different ideas about maths, and the children suffer. They don't know where they are.'

The whole area of parent–teacher relationships is riddled with misunderstandings.

What parents believe about teachers	What teachers believe about parents
'They aren't as good as they used to be.'	'They don't really appreciate or understand what goes on in schools.'
'They don't really understand my child.'	'Parents won't like or support change.'
'Teachers are too busy to be bothered with parents.'	'The parents we want to see never come to parents' evenings.'

Most teachers and parents will be able to provide other examples from their own experiences.

The relationship between teachers and parents is complex. Both groups have a strong commitment to the same children. Both teachers and parents have strong memories of their own schooling. Both groups can be vulnerable and easily threatened. It is not surprising that such misunderstandings exist when useful and effective communication is so difficult to achieve. Whenever there is a lack of communication, suspicion and anxiety are likely to occur. Interestingly, these tensions are still evident when teachers themselves are parents. This mathematics teacher writes about his concern when he thought his daughter might be about to be placed in a low set in the subject:

> 'My wife phoned a friend whose children were older and at the school. Yes, Mr Johns took lower ability children in Year 8 when they were in it. Yes, there were eight groups – apparently by abilities – when they were in it. It could have changed ...

> Why did we not phone Mr Johns? I don't know why there is this resistance to initiating such contacts, but it is there. Perhaps it is to do with the feeling that it will draw too much attention to my daughter, and that the teachers will not handle this sensitively.

> I don't want to be labelled a "fussy parent". If this had been the primary school I would have gone in. Why is there a greater "distance" between teachers and parents at secondary level?'

The cumulative effect of the lack of parent–teacher dialogue and involvement can lead to very negative attitudes. Often parents feel that the only channel open to them is to write to the school. This distressing letter from a parent is an example in which a number of resentments are aired together:

> 'Owen has not done his homework as we cannot understand just what he has to do.

> I would like to know what finding monkeys in trees has to do with maths, therefore I would be grateful if in future you could give him maths homework and not silly party games.

> If this is the standard, no wonder children are leaving school unable to read, write or do maths. Maybe before striking for more pay and so on you would do the job you're paid for.'

Often teachers cite parents as a reason for not implementing curriculum change. Frequently they are concerned about parents' preconceptions as to what mathematics should be about. For example two teachers wrote:

> 'Parental anxiety in respect of the education of their children is very natural and they will resent any change from what they regard as the "right" or "accepted" way of doing maths.'

> 'Parents like to see books with "sums" they can understand and lots of ticks.'

We have found, however, that when teachers are themselves more confident about why they are changing their approach in the classroom, parental involvement is welcomed. Teachers wrote:

'Remember parents care, are anxious, and will be your greatest ally if their children enjoy maths and don't feel it's a waste of time.'

'Whatever we do it has to be a two-way process where teachers have open minds too. We should learn from each other.'

> **STATEMENT 34**
> No sustained change can be effected unless parents are involved in, aware of and support the developments taking place. Excluding parents is to deny a large part of the experience that pupils bring with them to school.

Schools do make many efforts to communicate with parents, with varied amounts of success. For most parents and teachers, contact is made only at consultative evenings and therefore parents get little chance to appreciate the nature of the changes involved in mathematics teaching and learning. When specific mathematics evenings are held, they are often about no more than passing on information, consisting of lectures from heads of departments followed by questions from the more articulate and confident parents. We have found that more useful involvement is achieved through parents themselves taking part in mathematical activities, thereby experiencing the positive aspects of the subject. A teacher proposed:

'It is necessary to encourage parents to participate in the changed curriculum in order that they do not feel in the dark or threatened.

Meetings need to be occasions where parents can take part in activities. In short, we need to involve parents to gain their support.'

Where this kind of direct involvement has been encouraged, parents have become very positive in their support of developments in mathematics teaching.

The following quotations are from parents who wrote of their feelings after attending a day in their children's school doing mathematics and talking with teachers. This day was the first of what has become a regular occurrence.

'I thoroughly enjoyed my day at school because I found the methods of learning much more interesting than when I was at school.'

'There was more than one way of solving some of the problems. You had to use your initiative and put forward different ideas to come up with the right answers.'

'I was pleasantly surprised to find that school mathematics involved a much more interesting and brain-teasing set of problems to solve.'

'I enjoyed the challenge of solving problems.'

'There was an air of good humour among the parents, who for the most part were total strangers to each other when we first arrived, but who I'm sure by the end of the day became very good friends.'

'The work was very different from my own school work of 20 years ago. I had to think for myself, instead of copying work from the board.'

'At the beginning of the morning I felt a slight reluctance to try anything, and thought that a child with little confidence would feel the same. However, as I progressed and got over the first hurdle, my confidence increased and I became very absorbed in the questions.'

'I can now see how teaching methods will relate to the new exams, which will get pupils to think, rather than to learn parrot fashion.'

There are many strategies for facilitating this kind of parental involvement. Some which teachers have used and found to be successful are indicated below.

- Inviting pupils to explain to parents.
  One parent commented that hearing his daughter go through what she had done enabled him to appreciate how much thinking and problem solving had gone into the work.

- Sending work home to be done by the pupils with their parents.
  This not only allows parents to experience the type of work their children are doing but can also serve to open up communication. A teacher wrote:

    'Justin had taken a problem home with him that he couldn't do in class. The next day he said, "Miss, you know that puzzle we were doing yesterday? Well I gave it to my mum to do and she took simply ages!" It had obviously boosted Justin's confidence.'

- Inviting parents to work alongside pupils on some mathematics.

- Inviting parents into school for the day.
  Two parents wrote after such a day:

    'I would definitely like to repeat the process, perhaps regularly.'

    'I was stimulated and motivated to come again.'

- Encouraging pupils to run mathematical sessions for the parents.

- Presenting parents with contrasting methods of teaching the same things.
  On one evening parents were given a worksheet on long multiplication to complete. They were then invited to explore multiplication patterns on a table-square. In both cases, there was a need to perform multiplication sums, and for many parents the richness of the table-square approach was highlighted.

- Asking parents who are already involved to run sessions and get other parents involved.

Direct involvement is essential in gaining the support of employers as well as parents. It is only when this involvement is taking place that the full potential of community support can be realized. The potential is indeed great, when it is considered what facilities are available. The following ideas, some of which have been tried, were part of the project's agenda for action:

- Exhibitions in local community centres such as libraries, leisure centres, town halls and so on. Some teachers have found it beneficial to have pupils running the displays, talking about their work and inviting involvement.

- Family mathematics workshops held in community centres.

- 'Ideal Home'-type mathematics exhibitions consisting of workshops, including the use of computers and electronics devices, displays of equipment and chances to use them, discussion groups and videos with realistic strategies for follow-ups.

- Regular local radio and television 'mathematics spots'.

- Joint mathematics workshops with local artisans. Frequently people do not realize how much mathematics there is in their profession or craft, and how much mathematics they already know.

One parent said:

'My husband will be delighted to know that what he is doing is maths. He always thought he was bad at it.'

Most of what is advocated here would not be considered unusual in other areas of the curriculum; for example, local history, recreation and sport, science and technology. Failure to consider mathematics as worthy of such events is often because of the lack of awareness about the presence of mathematics in these activities and also the lack of appreciation of the subject's intrinsic fascination. This appreciation can only come through the active involvement outlined earlier in this chapter.

The initiatives for the types of mathematics community project proposed here must not come solely from teachers. Parents, local employers and local councils all have a responsibility to help raise awareness through, for example, the discussion of the issues at local committees, as well as offering accommodation, skills, display facilities, publicity and manpower.

SUMMARY

The Situation

- The whole area of parent–teacher relationships is riddled with misunderstandings because of a lack of communication.

- Useful and effective communication is difficult to achieve because of the complex nature of the relationship between parents and teachers.

- The cumulative effect of the lack of parent–teacher dialogue and involvement can lead to very negative attitudes.

- Often teachers cite parents as reasons for not implementing curriculum change. Frequently they are concerned about parents' preconceptions as to what mathematics should be about.

- When teachers are themselves more confident about why they are changing their approach in the classroom, parental involvement is more likely to be welcomed.

- No sustained change can be effected unless parents are involved in, aware of and support the developments taking place. Excluding parents is to deny a large part of the experience that pupils bring with them to school.

- When specific mathematics evenings are held, they are often about no more than passing on information, consisting of lectures from heads of departments followed by questions from the more articulate and confident parents.

- Where the kind of active involvement outlined in this chapter has been achieved, parents have become very positive in their support of developments in mathematics teaching.

Recommendations

- More useful parental involvement must be achieved through parents taking part in mathematical activities themselves thereby experiencing the positive aspects of the subject.

- It is essential that any initiative designed to involve parents is not seen as a one-off activity. If effective and useful communication is to be achieved, such involvement must be on a regular basis.

- Direct involvement is essential in gaining the support of employers as well as parents.

- In addition to school-focused activities, initiatives need to be made widespread throughout the community.

- The initiatives for mathematics community projects cannot come solely from teachers. Parents, local employers and local councils all have a responsibility to help raise awareness.

ENDNOTE

* Throughout this chapter the term 'parent' has been used to include parents and carers.

Chapter 10

Epilogue

In conversations and discussions, we have found that certain misconceptions have arisen with regard to the project and its work. Some examples are given below.

It had been said that:	**We are saying that:**
Our main aim is that pupils and teachers should enjoy their mathematics lessons more. *See:* *Chapter 2, 'Children learning mathematics'*	Our main aim is that pupils should attain a higher standard in the subject, and the strategies we advocate to achieve this certainly generate greater motivation, enjoyment and confidence. These positive attitudes to mathematics are a major factor in enabling pupils to achieve greater success and to apply their knowledge and skills to other areas of their life.
We think you can learn everything by 'investigations'. *See:* *Chapter 2, 'Children learning mathematics'* *Chapter 6, 'Schemes'*	'Investigations' must not be seen as new 'topics' to be covered on top of existing syllabus work. An enquiry approach – inviting pupils to question, challenge, discuss, interpret and explore – should pervade *all* mathematics learning. Conventional 'topics' such as percentages, trigonometry or algebra are rich areas for this kind of exploration.
We think children should never be helped or told what to do by their teacher. *See:* *Chapter 2, 'Children learning mathematics'*	Teachers have a responsibility to act as catalysts in order to ensure that opportunities exist for children to take greater responsibility for their own learning. Pupils need to be encouraged to challenge their assumptions and develop their own strategies for dealing with mathematics. The teacher's role is essential here in helping pupils through stimulating, coordinating, focusing, challenging, supporting and facilitating.

We think teachers need only administrative help from advisers and other in-service providers – that all teacher development needs is a room with a kettle where teachers can 'work together'.
See:
Chapter 4, 'Teacher development'

In-service providers have a responsibility to act as catalysts in order to ensure that opportunities exist for teachers to take greater responsibility for their own development. Teachers need to be encouraged to challenge their assumptions and develop their own strategies for dealing with their own particular classrooms. The in-service provider's role is essential here in helping teachers through stimulating, co-ordinating, focusing, challenging, supporting and facilitating.

The classroom approaches we advocate need 'special' teachers.
See:
Chapter 4, 'Teacher development'

All teachers can become more confident and effective in the classroom. It is often the case that when teachers begin to work together and become more successful, they are seen and reclassified as 'special' teachers.

Class size is not one of our concerns.
See:
Chapter 4, 'Teacher development'
Chapter 7, 'Working across the curriculum'

An improvement in the staff–pupil ratio is important. As teaching is such an isolated job, rather than a simple reduction in class size, it will be more beneficial in many cases to use the improved ratio to encourage collaborative teaching (for example, two teachers working together with one larger class).

We expect teachers to give up a good deal of their free time.
See:
Chapter 1, 'Introduction'
Chapter 4, 'Teacher development'

Money and time for regular teacher release work both in and out of school is essential for the kind of teacher development advocated by the project. Creative timetabling can also allow development work with colleagues to take place in school time on a regular basis.

We think all development must be 'bottom up', beginning with teachers in the classroom, and that senior management have no part to play in the process.
See:
Chapter 3, 'Aims and actions'
Chapter 4, 'Teacher development'
Chapter 5, 'Widespread, sustained curriculum development'
Chapter 7, 'Working across the curriculum'

Improvements and change can only be sustained if teachers in the classroom believe in and support the developments taking place. Senior management has a positive, creative role to play. Their active involvement and organizational support are essential to sustain initiatives.

Our dissemination depends on a small group of apparently successful and enthusiastic individuals.
See:
Chapter 5, 'Widespread, sustained curriculum development'

Dissemination must always be firmly rooted in the personal experiences of teachers in their classrooms. This is achieved through a constantly growing and developing network of personal contact and involvement – a cellular growth model of expansion. This is a long-term, continuous process.

We think publishing 'schemes' cannot bring about widespread improvement in the quality of children's mathematics learning.
See:
Chapter 5, 'Widespread, sustained curriculum development'
Chapter 6, 'Schemes'

We think publishing 'schemes' cannot bring about widespread improvement in the quality of children's mathematics learning.

We think published schemes and guidelines have no place in a mathematics department.
See:
Chapter 6, 'Schemes'

Where such schemes are used and recognized as vehicles for staff development they may be useful. However, they cannot short cut the longer-term investment in teacher development that is necessary, and may actually inhibit the process.

We think assessment always inhibits the learning process.
See:
Chapter 8 'Evaluating and assessing mathematics'

Sensitive assessment schemes must be an integral part of the work going on in the classroom, and hence support the mathematics curriculum. Therefore pupils should be actively involved in their own assessment and fully understand the process.

The changes in mathematics teaching we advocate will not be supported by parents.
See:
Chapter 9, 'Parents'

When parents are directly involved in, and aware of, the developments taking place in the classroom, they actively support the work their children are doing in mathematics.

Some project reflections

The following illustrations demonstrate the quality of the developments brought about by those involved in the project network.

1 **Pupils are achieving greater success in the subject.**
   This is true of pupils across the age and ability range in terms of both traditional examination success and their enjoyment, motivation, confidence and interest in mathematics. Their perceptions of the subject have broadened enabling them to apply their knowledge and skills to other areas of their life.
   See Chapter 2, 'Children learning mathematics', and Chapter 8, 'Evaluating and assessing mathematics'.

2 **The number of pupils choosing to take mathematics at A level has increased.**
   See Chapter 2, 'Children learning mathematics'.

3 **Teachers are finding greater satisfaction in their classrooms.**
   They see their children using and discussing mathematics in ways they do not expect, and their own interest in the subject has been reawakened and broadened.
   See Chapter 4, 'Teacher development'.

4 **The work has not been limited to individual teachers' classrooms.**
   Departments are working together and in many cases senior management have facilitated developments through organizational initiatives and support.
   See Chapter 3, 'Aims and actions', and Chapter 4, 'Teacher development'.

5 **Teachers' views of their own professional responsibilities have widened.**
   They are, for example, more willing to take on issues concerning assessment initiatives, new technology and resourcing. Membership of the professional mathematical associations has increased in the region, with many teachers now actively contributing to journals and other publications for the first time in their careers.
   See Chapter 3, 'Aims and actions', and Chapter 4, 'Teacher development'.

6 **Teachers have become more discerning with regard to in-service provision, published material and other resources.**
   For example, they are not as willing to take on pre-packaged mathematics schemes when they see that the schemes do not encourage their pupils to develop mathematically through questioning, challenging, discussing, interpreting and exploring. Reference and practical materials, everyday articles and pupils' own interests are being used imaginatively in the classroom. Teachers are also more aware of the broad opportunities that exist with regard to mathematics learning within initiative such as GCSE and so on.
   See Chapter 4, ' Teacher development, Chapter 5, 'Widespread, sustained curriculum development', and Chapter 6, 'Schemes'.

7 **The enormous value of collaborative work between local authorities has been demonstrated by the project.**

The LA advisers had a common aim to involve more of their teachers and schools in the kind of professional development indicated throughout the report. Their co-operation, support and joint initiatives have been a major factor in the project's success.

See Chapter 5, 'Widespread, sustained curriculum development'.

8 **Support and working groups have been set up by teachers throughout the region.**

They serve two vital purposes in ensuring that: a) the teachers involved no longer feel isolated in their classrooms or schools and they learn from each other's experiences and b) their self-appraisal skills are developed through classroom experimentation, reflection and discussion. The groups provide an important follow up to courses run in the region and through them the work of the teachers involved has directly influenced the emphasis of subsequent courses and curriculum developments within the project authorities. The fact that the groups, once initiated, have been largely self-sustaining, flourished and have continued to grow throughout the period of the project (1983–86) illustrates the importance attached to them by teachers.

See Chapter 5, 'Widespread, sustained curriculum development'.

9 **The project has had great influence on mathematics in-service provision for GCSE.**

Teachers involved in the project network have been widely used to initiate developments concerning extended coursework, oral and practical work, changing the climate in the classroom and more general assessment issues. Interactive in-service material, produced by a group of teachers involved in the network, was widely used in schools across the country and overseas, on in-service courses and was recommended by the then Secondary Examinations Council.

See Chapter 5, 'Widespread, sustained curriculum development' and Chapter 8, 'Evaluating and assessing mathematics'.

10 **The project has begun to have far-reaching effects across the curriculum.**

Cooperative teaching between subjects has taken place and has resulted in greater understanding of common learning and teaching problems and aims.

See Chapter 7, 'Working across the curriculum'.

11 **Teachers have found that actively involving parents in the developments taking place has led to increased support.**

This has greatly benefited the pupils.

See Chapter 9, 'Parents and carers'.

12 **The project has enabled teachers within the network to devise and contribute to a wide range of booklets containing ideas, strategies and case studies.**

Although the production of material was not central to the project's work, these resources proved popular because of their relevance to classroom life and their interactive in-service potential.

See Chapter 6, 'Schemes'.

We have identified a shorter list of books that have particularly influenced the project team.

Abercrombie, M. L. J. (1969) *The Anatomy of Judgement*, London: Pelican

Ahmed, A., Williams, H. and Wickham, G. (2002) *Numeracy Activities*, Key Stage 3, Stafford: Network Educational Press

APU (1980–) *Mathematical Development: Secondary and Primary Reports*, London: HMSO

Association of Teachers of Mathematics (ATM) (1969) *Notes of Mathematics in Primary Schools*, Cambridge University Press

ATM (1977) *Notes of Mathematics for Children*, Cambridge: Cambridge University Press

ATM (1970) *Mathematical Reflections*, Cambridge: Cambridge University Press

ATM (1980) *Language and Mathematics*, Derby: ATM

ATM (1966) *The Development of Mathematical Activity in Children*, Derby: ATM

Bateson, G. (1973) *Steps to an Ecology of Mind*, London: Paladin

Beer, S. (1975) *Platform for Change*, New York: Wiley

Bell, A. W., Costello, J. and Kuchemann, D. (1983) *A Review of Research in Mathematical Education. Part A: Research on Learning and Teaching Mathematics*, London: NFER-Nelson

Bishop, A. J. and Nickson, M. (1983) *A Review of Research in Mathematical Education. Part B: Research on the Social Context of Mathematics Education*, London: NFER-Nelson

Blanchard, J. (1986) *Out in the Open*, Cambridge: Cambridge University Press

Board of Education (1905) *Suggestions for the Consideration of Teachers*, HMSO

Board of Education (1912) *The Teaching of Mathematics in the United Kingdom. Parts I and II*, HMSO

Board of Education (1937) *Handbook of Suggestions for Teachers*, HMSO

Brookes, W. M. and Underwood, V. L. (1970) *Development in Mathematical Education*, School of Education Southampton, Derby: ATM

Burgess, R. G. (1985) *Issues in Educational Research Qualitative Methods*, London: Falmer Press

Carr, W. and Kemmis, S. (1986) *Becoming Critical*, London: Falmer Press

Cockcroft, W. H. (Chairman) (1982) *Mathematics Counts: Report of the Committee of Enquiry*, London: HMSO

Collingwood, R. G. (1970) *An Autobiography*, Oxford: Oxford University Press

Davis, P. J. and Hersh, R. (1981) *The Mathematical Experience*, London: Pelican

DES (1979) *Aspects of Secondary Education*, London: HMSO

DES (1980) *A View of the Curriculum*, London: HMSO

DES (1984) *Slow Learning and Less Successful Pupils in Secondary Schools*, London: DES

DES (1985) *Mathematics from 6 to 16: Curriculum Matters 3*, London: HMSO

DES (1985) *Curriculum from 5 to 16*, London: HMSO

DES (1985) *Technology and School Science*, London: HMSO

DES (1985) *Better Schools*, London: DES

Dickson L , Brown M and Gibson O (1984) *Children Learning Mathematics*, Orlando: Holt, Rinehart and Winston

Donaldon, M. (1978) *Children's Minds*, London: Fontana

Fitzgerald, A. (1985) *New Technology and Mathematics in Employment*, London: DES

Fletcher, T. J. (HMI) (1983) *Microcomputers and Mathematics in Schools*, London: DES

Freudenthal, H. (1978) *Weeding and Sowing*, Boston: D. Reidel Publishing Company

Gattegno, C. (1970) *What we owe Children*, London: Routledge and Kegan Paul

Gattegno, C. (1963) *For the Teaching of Mathematics, vol. 1*, Fishguard: Educational Explorers Ltd

Hargreaves, D. H. (1972) *Interpersonal Relations and Education*, London: Routledge and Kegan Paul

Hargreaves, D. H. (Chairman) (1984) *Improving Secondary Schools*, Swindon: Swindon Press Ltd

Hart, K. (ed.) (1981) *Children's Understanding of Mathematics: 11–16*, London: John Murray

Heidegger, M. (1978) *Basic Writings*, London: Routledge and Kegan Paul

HMI (1982) *Mathematics in the Sixth Form*, London: HMSO

HMI (1976) *Mathematics, Science and Modern Language – An Appraisal*, London: DES

Holt, J. (1969) *How Children Fail*, London: Pelican

Howson, A. G. (1983) *A Review of Research in Mathematical Education. Part C: Curriculum Development and Curriculum Research*, London: NFER-Nelson

Kline, M. (1953) *Mathematics in Western Culture*, Oxford: Oxford University Press

Krutetskii, V. A. (1976) *The psychology of mathematical abilities in school children*, Chicago: University of Chicago Press

Lakatos, I. (1976) *Proofs and refutations: the logic of mathematical discovery*, Cambridge: Cambridge University Press

London County Council (1911) *The Teaching of Arithmetic in London Elementary Schools*, London: LCC

Macnab, D. S. and Cummine, J. A. (1986) *Teaching mathematics 11–16*, Oxford: Basil Blackwell

Ministry of Education (1958) *Teaching mathematics in secondary schools*, Pamphlet no 36, London: HMSO

Morgan, J. (1977) *Affective Consequences for the Learning and Teaching of Mathematics of an Individual Learning Programme*, Stirling: University of Stirling

Monteith, A. (1928) *The Teaching of Arithmetic*, Edinburgh: Harrap

Oldknow, A. and Smith, D. (1983) *Learning Mathematics with Micros*, Chichester: Ellis Horwood Ltd

Oldknow, A. (1985) *Graphics with Microcomputers*, London: Nelson

Papert, S. (1980) *Mindstorms: Children, Computers and Powerful Ideas*, New York: Basic Books Inc

Polanyi, M. (1962) *Personal Knowledge*, London: Routledge and Kegan Paul

Popper, K. R. (1978) *Conjectures and Refutations*, London: Routledge and Kegan Paul

Rowntree, D. (1977) *Assessing Students: How shall we know them?* New York: Harper and Row

Rutter, M. et al. (1979) *Fifteen Thousand Hours: Secondary Schools and Their Effects on Children*, London: Open Books

Schools Council (1977) *Match and Mismatch*, Edinburgh: Oliver and Boyd

Schools Council (1977) *Mixed Ability Teaching in Mathematics*, London: Evans/Methuen Educational

Sewell, B. (1962) *The Use of Mathematics by Adults in Daily Life*, Leicester: Advisory Council for Adult and Continuing Education

Stenhouse, L. (1975) *An Introduction to Curriculum Research and Development*, London: Heinemann

Tahta, D. G. (ed.) (1972) *A Boolean Anthology: Selected Writings of Mary Boole*, Derby: ATM

Waddington, C. H. (1977) *Tools for Though*, London: Paladin

Wertheimer, M. (1961) *Productive Thinking*, London: Tavistock

Whitehead, A. N. (1932) *The Aims of Education*, Edinburgh: Williams and Norgate

Wittgenstein, L. (1976) *Philosophical Investigations*, Oxford: Basil Blackwell

Wittgenstein, L. (1977) *On Certainty*, Oxford: Basil Blackwell

Yates, J. (1978) *Four Mathematical Classrooms*, Southampton: University of Southampton

The following select periodicals also contain many important and relevant articles.

Educational Studies in Mathematics, Boston: D. Reidel Publishing Company
For the Learning of Mathematics, Vancouver: FLM Publishing Association
Mathematics in School, Harlow: Longman Group Ltd on behalf of the Mathematical Association
Mathematics Teaching, Derby: ATM
Micromaths, Oxford: ATM and Basil Blackwell
Struggle, London: ILEA and the Mathematical Association
Support for Learning – Successor to Remedial Education, Journal of NARE

SECTION C: Supporting publications

The following publications are directly associated with the project. They include publications arising from the work of primary teachers involved with the project. They take the form of booklets, working papers and in-service resources.

Ahmed, A. G., 'Implications of the Cockcroft Report, in mathematics for all, science and technology education no. 20', UNESCO (also published separately by WSIHE as 'Foundations of Mathematics for all')

Ahmed, A. G. and Bufton N. (co-directors), 'Teachers evaluating and assessing mathematics (TEAM)', Southern Region Examination Board/WSIHE

Ahmed, A. and Williams, H. (1992) 'The Raising Achievement in Mathematics Project report', WSIHE

Ahmed, A. G., Biddle, A., Savage, C., Smith T. and Vowles, L., 'Mathematics for low attainers', WSIHE/West Sussex County Council

Bird, M., 'Beginning investigations', WSIHE

Bird, M., 'Generating mathematical activity in the classroom', Mathematical Association

Bird, M., 'Mathematics with 7 and 8 year olds, 8 and 9 year olds and 10 and 11 year olds', Mathematical Association (available as separate booklets)

Bufton, N. and Smith, D., 'CHIMPS – Computer help in mathematics problem solving', WSIHE

Evans, K., 'Needs in the mathematics classroom – a study of fourth year low attaining pupils', WSIHE

Low Attainers Mathematics Project (LAMP), 'Advisory teachers' discussion document', WSIHE

LAMP, 'Changes', WSIHE

LAMP, 'What is mathematics all about?', WSIHE

LAMP, 'Schemes', WSIHE

LAMP, 'Parents', WSIHE

Oldknow, A., 'Some powerful short programs', WSIHE

Oldknow, A., 'Some more short maths programs', WSIHE

Oldknow, A., White, J. and Cross, J., 'Conic sections', WSIHE

Pinel, A., Sharpe, R. and Ellis, R. (eds), 'Making a start', WSIHE

Pinel, A., 'Mathematical activity tile handbook', WSIHE

Smith, D., 'PUMAS – Primary children understanding mathematics through microcomputer activities in schools', WSIHE

Smith, D., 'CAMELS – Computer activities in mathematics learning strategies', WSIHE

Tagart, C., 'Small changes in my classroom', WSIHE

Waddingham, J. and Wigley, A. (eds), 'Secondary mathematics with micros in-service pack', MEP National Mathematical Panel

The following Open University video materials contain a significant contribution from some of the project schools:

Secondary Mathematics: Classroom Practice, (PM644) BBC/OU

Working Mathematically with Low Attainers: Turning 'I can't' into 'I can and I did', BBC/OU and the Mathematical Association

In addition to all the above publications, much of the material associated with the project existed as a bank of 'working archives'. These were in the form of videos, audio tapes, personal diaries and more substantial case studies. From time to time edited selections from these were published as articles, pamphlets and in-service resources.

Those associated with the project continued to contribute to various courses and conferences both nationally and internationally.

Index

A

accommodation, classroom, 58, 59
advisory teams, 40
    see also in-service provision; teacher
        development
aims, 27–32, 43–5, 48, 75
    hidden, 28–30
    of LAMP, 2–3, 9
    mismatch with actions, 27–8
assessment, 49
    criteria, developing departmental, 6, 37,
      42, 67
    diagnostic incompatibilities, 72–3
    of investigative work, 37–8
    learning process, part of, 71
    pupils' perceptions, 70
    reasons for, 69
    responsibility for, 74, 75
    self-evaluation, pupils', 72, 77
    teacher development, 87–88
    timed written tests and examinations, 71

B

beliefs and perceptions
    dominant convictions, 33–4
    in-service providers, 40–41, 45
    mathematics, 11, 24, 34
    parents', 10, 72, 80–1, 84
    pupils', 3, 8–10, 87–8
    teachers', 2–4, 8, 14–15, 30, 49–50, 56–7

C

classroom strategies, 19–20, 36, 644–5
    see also learning mathematics; teacher
        development
Cockcroft Committee Report, 2
    Foundation list, 33
    investigative work, 18, 24
    involvement, 28
community involvement, 83–4

    see also parents
computers, 1, 4, 58, 59, 83
    software packages, 54
co-operative teaching, 37, 89
cross-curricular links, 61, 68
curriculum development, 3
    detachment, 44–5
    dissemination, 46, 51
    LAMP recommendations, 36, 40, 51
    previous projects, 90
    teachers' responsibility for, 43, 47, 50
    see also schemes

D

development, 3, 43–4, 68, 78–81, 87 8
    curriculum, *see* curriculum development
        mathematical, 1, 3, 8, 14–15, 18, 39,
          43, 56, 62–3, 72, 77
    LAMP recommendations, 4–6, 24,
    27–30, 32, 86
    teacher, see teacher development
diagnostic assessment, 71, 77
diet for low attainers, 3, 11
dissemination, 3, 46, 49–51, 87

E

employers, 1, 5, 71, 73, 77, 83–4
    see also parents
evaluation see assessment
examinations, 1–3, 15, 41, 75, 89
    see also assessment

F

facilitators, 38

G

GCSE (General Certificate of Secondary
    Education), 38, 89

H

headteachers/senior management, 56, 59, 86–87
  involvement, 31, 32, 63, 68
  views, 59
home-made schemes, 53, 56, 59

I

in-service provision, 41
networks, models of, 40, 89
providers beliefs, 43–4
see also teacher development
inhibitors, 56, 62–3
investigation, 18, 24, 46, 53, 85

L

LAMP (Low Attainers in Mathematics Project), 23, 47
  aims, 2–3, 91
  background, 91
  dissemination, 47
learning mathematics, 7
  changes in, 10, 23–4
  investigations, 18
  misconceptions, 85–87
  parental involvement, 80–82
  resources, 89
  schemes, 56, 87
  teacher development, 8, 39
  research process, 1
  review of project, 24
  teacher-researchers, 6
low attainment
  diet and, 3, 11
  lack of challenge, 12, 24

M

Mathematics from 5 to 16, 29
  see also beliefs and perceptions

N

networks, 49–51, 86–7, 87–9
non-specialist teachers of mathematics, 3, 55

O

organizational systems, 38, 41, 43, 57, 87
  see also schemes

P

parents, 1, 5, 11, 71, 79–84
LAMP recommendations, 49, 87–9
perceptions of mathematics, 9, 72
teacher development, 37–8
perceptions see beliefs and perceptions
published schemes, 53–4, 57, 59–60, 87

R

RAMP (Raising Achievement in Mathematics Project), 19
research process, 2–4
resources, 2, 53, 56–60, 94
  commercial, 3
  cross-curricular, 64
  LAMP recommendations 88–9
    and investment, 46
  personal, 37–9, 41
    and priority, 31

S

schemes, 1
  answer orientated, 62–3
  assessment, 75
  development, 39, 43
  home-made, 53, 56, 63
  investigatory elements, 63
  LAMP recommendations, 63, 87–88
  published, 53, 62
  resources, use of, 61
  software packages, 54
  teacher development, vehicle for, 34–6, 41, 54–55
  see also curriculum development
self-evaluation, pupils, 71, 75
senior management *see* headteachers
  support groups, 43–4, 49
  see also in-service provision, teacher development
syllabus, 11, 16–17, 24, 27, 30, 62, 85
  geography, 65
    and pressure, 1, 53, 62–3
    and teacher development, 33–4

T

teacher development, 32, 36
  assumptions, challenging, 40, 41, 85
  classroom strategies, evolving, 56–8
  LAMP recommendations, 86–87

time for, 36, 87
  see also in service provision
teacher researchers, 2–3, 40
tests, 3, 20, 38, 44–8, 68, 70, 71–72, 75–77
thematic approach, 62, 68
  see also cross-curricular links
timetabling, 40, 63, 68, 86